# Editing Eighteenth Century Novels

CONFERENCE ON EDITORIAL PROBLEMS

Conferences and Publications

1965 *Editing Sixteenth Century Texts*, ed. R. J. Schoeck (1966)
1966 *Editing Nineteenth Century Texts*, ed. John M. Robson (1967)
1967 *Editing Eighteenth-Century Texts*, ed. D. I. B. Smith (1968)
1968 *Editor, Author and Publisher*, ed. Wm. J. Howard (1969)
1969 *Editing Twentieth Century Texts*, ed. Francess G. Halpenny (1972)
1970 *Editing Seventeenth Century Prose*, ed. D. I. B. Smith (1972)
1971 *Editing Texts of the Romantic Period*, ed. John D. Baird (1972)
1972 *Editing Canadian Texts*, ed. Francess G. Halpenny (1975)
1973 *Editing Eighteenth Century Novels*, ed. G. E. Bentley, Jr. (1975)
1974 Editing Late Nineteenth Century Texts, convenor Eric W. Domville (University of Toronto)
1975 Editing Renaissance Plays, convenor Ann Lancashire (University of Toronto)

Copies of the publications through 1969 are available from the University of Toronto Press. Publications from 1970 are available from the Order Department of A. M. Hakkert Ltd., 125 Bermondsey Road, Toronto, Canada M4A 1X3.

# Editing
# Eighteenth Century
# Novels

Papers on Fielding, Lesage,
Richardson, Sterne, and Smollett
given at the
Conference on Editorial Problems
University of Toronto
November 1973

Edited by G. E. Bentley, Jr.

Published for
The Committee for The Conference on Editorial Problems
by A. M. Hakkert Ltd., Toronto, 1975

Published for The Committee for
The Conference on Editorial Problems by
A. M. Hakkert Ltd.
554 Spadina Crescent, Toronto, Canada M5S 2J9

Printed and bound in Canada

Library of Congress Catalogue Card Number 74-84099
Standard Book Number 88866-558-X

*To D. I. B. Smith*

# Contents

# Contributors

MARTIN C. BATTESTIN, Professor of English at the University of Virginia, is the author of *The Moral Basis of Fielding's Art* and the editor of Fielding's major novels for the Wesleyan Edition. His book, *The Providence of Wit: Aspects of Form in Augustan Literature and the Arts*, will be published this year by the Clarendon Press.

G. E. BENTLEY, Jr., Professor of English at University College, University of Toronto, is the editor of William Blake's *Vala or The Four Zeas* (1964), *Tiriel* (1967), *Writings* (in the press), and *America* (in the press), author of *The Early Engravings of Flaxman's Classical Designs* (1964), and *Blake Records* (1969), and compiler of *A Blake Bibliography* (with M. K. Nurmi, 1964; a revised edition as *Blake Books* by GEB is in the press) and of *The Blake Collection of Mrs Landon K. Thorne* (1971).

O M BRACK, Jr., Professor of English at Arizona State University, is general editor and textual editor for the Bicentennial Edition of the Works of Tobias Smollett. He is co-author of *Samuel Johnson's Early Biographers*

(1971), co-editor of *Bibliography and Textual Criticism: English and American Literature 1700 to the Present* (1969), *Henry Fielding's PASQUIN* (1973), and *Early Biographies of Samuel Johnson* (1974). He has also edited John Hoole's *Death of Johnson* (1972).

JOHN CARROLL, Chairman of the Department of English, University College, University of Toronto, editor of *Selected Letters of Samuel Richardson* (1964), is preparing an edition of *Clarissa* for the Oxford English Novels series.

ROGER LAUFER, Professor of French Literature, Université de Paris — VIII (Vincennes), was educated at the Sorbonne, the Ecole Normale Supérieure, the University of Liverpool and Yale University. He is the author of *Style Rococo, Style des "Lumiéres"* (1963), *Lesage, ou le métier de romancier* (1971), and *Introduction à la Textologie* (1972). He had edited Montfaucon de Villars' *Le Comte de Gabalis* (1963) and Lesage's *Le Diable Boiteux* (1970) with an *Etude de Bibliographie Matérielle*. His edition of Lesage's *Gil Blas de Santillane* awaits publication.

MELVYN NEW, Associate Professor of English at the University of Florida, has degrees from Columbia University and Vanderbilt University. He is the author of *Laurence Sterne as Satirist: A Reading of Tristram Shandy* (1969), and has published on Sterne in *PMLA, Modern Languages Quarterly*, and other journals. He is general editor of the Sterne edition as well as textual editor for *Tristram Shandy*.

# Editing Eighteenth Century Novels

# Introduction

# G. E. Bentley, Jr.

Scholarly editing is a craft or mystery long performed in private, whose apprentices, journeymen, and masters are rarely able to assemble for professions of the true faith. It is often surprising to isolated editors to discover in discussion with others how extensive is the community of knowledge, understanding, and technique of their craft.

The ninth Conference on Editorial Problems held at The University of Toronto on November 2nd and 3rd, 1973 gathered together true believers, along with a few heretics, from far and wide, from Ontario and Arizona, British Columbia and Florida, Nova Scotia and Utah, Texas and Paris, and from the provinces and states adjoining Ontario. The subject, novels of the Eighteenth Century, was one which has long been neglected, to the scandal of the faithful and the impoverishment of scholarship and criticism. At a time when masterful editions of drama are matters of course, from Shakespeare and Jonson to Congreve, Sheridan, and Yeats, when there are serious scholarly editions of most great poets of the Restoration and Eighteenth Century such as Dryden, Pope, Goldsmith, Johnson, and Blake, when even the essays of Addison and

Steele and Goldsmith and Johnson are printed in meticulously accurate texts, it is a matter for astonishment that
novels of the Eighteenth Century have been so largely
neglected. Considering only the four greatest Eighteenth
Century English novelists, Richardson, Fielding, Smollett,
and Sterne, it is very striking that there is in print no
collected edition of the works of any of them with which
modern scholars can be satisfied, and indeed only a very
few of their novels have appeared yet in anything like
reliable texts. The massive and mounting criticism of these
authors has therefore been based largely on unsatisfactory
or manifestly corrupt texts.

The correction of this lamentable situation is now well
under way, and at the 1973 Conference on Editorial
Problems we were extraordinarily fortunate to be able to
hear the editors of Richardson's *Clarissa* and Lesage's *Gil
Blas*[1] and the general editors of the works of Fielding,
Smollett, and Sterne. The presence of so many distinguished editors and auditors was in itself remarkable. The
study and the enjoyment of the best 18th Century novels
will be strikingly altered and enhanced when all the works
mooted at this Conference are in print. We owe a great
debt of gratitude to these editors, not least for their
willingness to discuss their trials and their triumphs with
us.

Though we concentrated on problems encountered in
one genre in one half-century — novels of about 1720 to
1770 — many of the issues discussed were perennial. The
collected editions of Fielding (edited by Professor Martin
Battestin), of Sterne (Melvyn New), and of Smollett (O M
Brack) are very large and diverse, including, for instance,
sermons, poems, and political tracts as well as novels, and
the time and energy devoted merely to organizing the
whole undertaking and finding collaborators was corre-

---

1. Indeed, *Gil Blas* was represented twice, for it will appear in a French
edition by Roger Laufer and in Smollett's English translation edited by O M
Brack. Professor Laufer has already edited Lesage's *Diable Boiteux* and
Professor Carroll has produced Richardson's *Selected Letters* (1964).

spondingly onerous, requiring years of effort. All these editions were initiated at a time when money for scholarly editions in North America was considerably more freely available than it is today,[2] and the scale on which they were conceived is generous and ambitious. For most of these editors, the essential interest of the work was critical, and such an interest is particularly visible in the concern for annotation of quotations and neologisms expressed by Professor Carroll. A less obvious though perhaps more time-consuming and basic activity is the collation of texts. For example, Professor New collated at least five copies of each of the nine volumes of the first edition of *Tristram Shandy* with his copytext, and, at a different stage of work, Professor Brack had ten editions of *Roderick Random* collated, and then four of these editions collated again. Thus far the work follows orthodox doctrine faithfully and labouriously.

The true editorial church for scholars of English Literature is founded on the scriptures particularly of Greg and Bowers, and, though it is not quite apostolic, it has seemed catholic for at least twenty years. Two of the most basic tenets of belief are that, in attempting to recreate the author's intentions as meticulously as possible in the absence of the manuscript copy prepared for the compositor, the editor should follow the first editon for "accidentals" affecting mere form such as spelling, punctuation, and capitalization, and reproduce the last edition corrected by the author for "substantives" of wording affecting content. In general, it is possible to establish clearly in individual cases the meaning of "first edition," "last authorized edition," "substantive," and "accidental," and the chief question is how, rather than whether, to follow the doctrine faithfully. Perfectly conscientious practise may permit some remarkable extensions of the doctrine, as when Professor Battestin produces a text for

2. Apparently only in Germany are scholarly editions initiated on such a generous scale in the 1970s.

the Man-of-the-Hill episode in *Tom Jones* which appeared
in no previous edition or manuscript, or when Professor
New bases part of the text of *Tristram Shandy* not on
Sterne's manuscript or on any contemporary edition of
*Tristram Shandy* but on the book by Deventer which
Sterne and his compositors were trying with increasing
fallibility to copy. This may seem ecclecticism run
rampant, but it accords with the scriptures well enough.

Heresy begins to creep in, however, with the question of
"accidentals" and the author's intention. According to
doctrine, the author rarely cared enough about minutiae of
punctuation and capitalization to correct his texts meticulously in this respect. Therefore, even when he revised
the second edition, say, the first edition probably reproduces his intentions in "accidentals" most faithfully. For
authors who are indifferent to such minutiae, the theory
works well enough.

But what of the author who deliberately conveys his
meaning in significant part through what we ordinarily call
"accidentals"? Fielding signals jokes and quotations
through italicization, and Sterne warned his printer not to
alter "one Comma or Tittle" and apparently tried to
control the very lengths of dashes in his printed text. For
Fielding, this amounts to what Professor Battestin calls
"substantive uses of typography." And if italics, capitals
dashes, and quotation marks are or may be substantive, the
distinction between "accidental" and "substantive" seems
to break down.

Indeed, when one considers the practise of editors in
other languages, it appears that the one true catholic
editorial church may be only an Anglican edifice sub-
scribed to by editors of the English-speaking world.
Professor Laufer, a French textologist of distinction,[3]
challenges the theortical bases of the distinction between
"accidentals" and "substantives," citing rival prophets

3. See Roger Laufer, *Introduction à la textologie:* vérification, établisse-
ment, édition des textes (Paris: Larousse, 1972).

particularly from France and Russia. He goes further and insists that the copytext must not only be emended to correct typographical errors, &c.; it must be modernized as well in areas such as punctuation, capitalization, and spelling, to make it accessible to students and scholars who are not specialists. (This is the opposite extreme from the German practise, which is to preserve the copytext inviolate, preserving even manifest typographical errors. The difference of practise extends to language. When speaking of alterations of clear typographical errors, the Anglicans say they are "correcting" a "corruption," whereas for the Germans the "correction" in the text is itself a corruption of the inviolable copytext.)[4] Professor Laufer goes further, citing Tomashevski's doctrine of "the unitary creative mood," and is willing to reject from the text (though not of course from his apparatus) an author's revisions made years after the publication of the first edition.

Here are challenges aplenty to the true editorial faith. Surely here is evidence to make us all dissenters, all Protestants, to remind us that each editorial problem is unique in context, requiring a fresh mind and fresh solutions. True philosophy will welcome any method of expressing effectively and with meticulous accuracy the author's intention to readers of our day. Truly, there are more editorial facts and methods than our philosophy has dreamed of. For reminding us that every editor must be priest and king in his own study, we should be grateful to the learned contributers to this volume.

The 1973 Toronto Conference on Editorial Problems was made possible by the scholarship of its speakers, by the continuing generosity of The Canada Council and of The University of Toronto, and by the devoted labours of

4. The Conference on Problems of Editing held at Bellagio, Italy, in September 1973, attended by Professors Bowers and Laufer and scholars from a dozen countries, made it apparent that the chief dichotomy of editorial practise was between the English-speaking world (followed in Holland, Belgium, France, Italy) and the German-speaking world. Perhaps the Russians form a third division.

its Committee consisting of G. E. Bentley, Jr., Professor
Hugo de Quehen, Professor Eric Domville, Mr. David
Esplin, Dean Francess Halpenny, Professor Ann Lancashire, Professor John McClelland, Principal John M.
Robson, Professor David Smith, and Professor D. I. B.
Smith. I should like to express here particularly my
gratitude to Don Smith, who was one of the begetters of
this Conference and who gave his energy to it with
characteristically selfless gaity from 1964 until 1973, when
he returned to a chair created for him in his native New
Zealand. We miss his levity and his wisdom.

15 December 1973                          G. E. Bentley, Jr
                              Convener (1973) and Chairman
                              Conference on Editorial Problems.

# Fielding's Novels
# and the Wesleyan Edition:
# Some Principles and Problems

## Martin Battestin

> They talk of *Principles*, but Notions prize,
> And All to one lov'd Folly Sacrifice.
>
> Pope

Considering the squibs and pasquils that have crackled in the pages of the *New York Review of Books* and the *TLS* since this Conference last turned its attention to the editing of eighteenth-century texts [1967], one is inclined to believe that nothing causes the academic gorge to rise quite so surely as the application in print of a rival theory of copy-text. The Textual Editor of the Wesleyan Fielding edition, who over a long and distinguished career has done much to introduce order and light into the inky regions of bibliographical studies, looms at the center of the controversy like Gulliver among the Lilliputians, the obvious target of those who would leave the business of editing to intuition rather than to science. To Edmund Wilson, who could recognize sublimity even in an adversary, Professor Bowers was nothing less than "the great Demiurge" of American editing.[1] To Donald Greene, whose polemical

---

1. "The Fruits of the MLA," *New York Review of Books*, 26 September 1968, p. 10.

9

talents run more to the bathos, he is merely the Dean of "the Virginia school"[2] – a title, one suspects, that Professor Bowers would modestly decline, since the "school" in question was founded by a Cantabrigian, Sir Walter Greg,[3] and comprises a numerous cosmoplitan body of editors on both sides of the Atlantic who acknowledge the cogency of Greg's by now classic theory of copy-text.

There is a certain appropriateness in Wilson's metaphor, since, like any self-respecting Demiurge, Professor Bowers has attempted to order this particular province of scholarly endeavor according to rational principle: to state a complex matter simply, this is the principle that, lacking the manuscript of the work in question, an editor wishing to preserve as far as possible the texture in which the author clothed his thoughts – the so-called "accidentals" of his style – must choose for his copy-text that edition of the work which stands closest to the original holograph, and must faithfully reproduce those features of the copy – capitalization, pointing, spelling, typographical variation, etc. – which determine its texture and which, therefore, subtly affect the reader's experience and understanding of the work. Even readers unskilled in the more esoteric aspects of bibliography – and I count myself among them – must acknowledge the reasonableness of this hypothesis, provided, of course, that the editor's objective is to establish a "definitive" text. Defending the very different treatment of accidentals in the Yale edition of Johnson, Professor Greene scoffs irreverently at this "hallowed doctrine," dismissing it as merely one of the "fashionable dogmatisms" of the moment. But there are sciences in which dogma (if, as in this instance, it is identical with a principle founded on common sense and proved by

2. "No Dull Duty: The Yale Edition of the Works of Samuel Johnson," in D.I.B. Smith, ed. *Editing Eighteenth-Century Texts*, Papers given at the Editorial Conference, University of Toronto, October 1967 (Toronto, 1968), 99-100. See also Greene's letter in *TLS*, 17 July 1969, p. 779.

3. See Greg's classic article, "The Rationale of Copy-Text," *Studies in Bibliography*, III (1950), 19-36.

common experience) is preferable to whimsy as a guide to
truth; bibliography is one such science. As an alternative to
Greg's method, the Yale editors tend to resort (since they
are inconsistent in this matter, one must speak of
tendencies) to the discredited policy of choosing as
copy-text the last edition revised by the author, by which
procedure the accumulated sophistications of various
compositors are preserved;[4] moreover, since the policy of
the edition is to modernize capitalization and pointing and
to alter italics to roman within quotation marks, the
editors inevitably introduce innumerable sophistications of
their own. This, as Professor Bowers has called it, who
anticipated Edmund Wilson in appreciating the mythic
dimension of contemporary bibliography, is the "Pan-
dora's box of partial modernization,"[5] a policy that
commits the editor to the impossible task of evolving a
"reliable" text by caprice and surmise. The distinction
between the two methods was succinctly stated shortly
before his death by John Crow:

> When a student or any reasonably literate reader reads
> Johnson, he should want the best available evidence of what
> Johnson wrote. In my view the first compositor is a better
> witness than a twentieth-century editor. He is an unconscious
> witness; he had an author's manuscript before him and he set
> type from it. He is a contemporary witness, not a two-
> centuries-later advocate.

The editors of the Wesleyan edition are with Mr. Crow in
preferring the evidence of the original compositor to the
"guesses" (or, to give them a more favourable construction, the "discriminations") of a present-day editor, how-

---

4. Consider, for example, the compounded corruption of the following
passage that resulted when the compositor of the second edition of *Joseph
Andrews* inadvertently dropped the words "know I" from his first-editon
copy-text (the passage occurs in Book III, Chapter x): *1st edn.* "No," said the
Poet, "you and the whole Town know I had Enemies; *2nd edn.* "No," said the
Poet, "you and the whole Town had Enemies; *3rd edn.* "No," said the Poet,
"you and the whole Town were Enemies; *4th edn.* "No," said the Poet, "you
and the whole Town were my Enemies;
5. See Prof. Bowers's important review of Vol. II of the Yale Johnson
edition, *Modern Philology*, LXI (1964), 298-309, esp. p. 301.

ever scrupulous and well-intentioned he may be:

> 'Where are the discriminations of yesteryear, Father?'
> — 'Take a look in Bentley's *Milton* and Warburton's *Shakespeare*, my boy.'[6]

It will be granted, surely, that the test and justification of any editorial system is its usefulness in making available to us, as readers, the full meaning of an author. The establishment of a reliable text is, in other words, the fundamental act of criticism. Any editor, therefore, will respect his author's words, the "substantives" of his text. What the proponents of modernized, or partially modernized, editions will not concede is what is plainly true of many eighteenth-century texts: that the meaning of the author also partially resides in certain features of the original accidentals. Having recently prepared for the "general reader" a partially modernized text of *Tom Jones* for the Riverside series,* I am only too well aware of the awkwardness of an editor's committing himself to a policy of reducing Fielding's capitals, for example — a policy, indeed, which Professor Todd, in an amusing metaphor applied to the Yale Johnson edition, regards as not merely awkward, but villainous: a "ruthless decapitalization behind the scenes."[7] As an illustration of the perils of this procedure, consider the dilemma of the modernizing editor who confronts the following passage in which Fielding states an important theme of *Tom Jones*:

> Prudence and Circumspection are necessary even to the best of Men. They are indeed as it were a Guard to Virtue, without which she can never be safe. It is not enough that your Designs, nay that your Actions are intrinsically good, you must take Care they shall appear so. If your Inside be never so beautiful, you must preserve a fair Outside also. This must be

* Since this essay went to press, the Riverside edition of *Tom Jones* has been cancelled for budgetary reasons.

6. See John Crew's letter in reply to Prof. Greene, *TLS*, 25 September 1969, pp. 1079-80.

7. See William B. Todd's review of the Yale Johnson edition, Vol. II, in *Philological Quarterly*, XLIII (1964), 368. Among others who have lamented the unfortunate consequences of the Yale policy of decapitalization, see Bowers in the article cited above (n. 5) and F. W. Bateson, *Review of English Studies*, New Ser., XVII (1966), 327-31.

constantly looked to, or Malice and Envy will take Care to
blacken it so, that the Sagacity and Goodness of an *Allworthy*
will not be able to see through it, and to discern the Beauties
within. Let this, my young Readers, be your constant Maxim,
That no Man can be good enough to enable him to neglect the
Rules of Prudence; nor will Virtue herself look beautiful,
unless she be bedecked with the outward Ornaments of
Decency and Decorum.[8]

Fielding's capitals in this passage achieve effects that have
subtle substantive implications: by raising abstract qualities to the level of personification, they supply a certain
color, a full-bodied richness, to the general precept he is
inculcating, or they function to emphasize crucial anti-
theses ("Inside" vs. "Outside") or parallelisms ("Decency
and Decorum"). Most of these effects will be lost in a
modernized text. The emphasis capitals certainly will go,
and, though the editor may wish to retain the capital for
"Virtue," which is a clear personification, he will probably
wish to reduce to lower case those other abstractions —
"Prudence," "Circumspection," "Malice," "Envy," "Sagacity," "Goodness" — which Fielding has personified in a
less prominent, almost subliminal way. For to capitalize all
the personifications here would, in a modernized text,
appear to the reader as a clumsy and distracting anomaly.
Equally unfortunate is the insidious adulteration of tone
and texture that results from the effort to "normalize"
Fielding's original punctuation in the novel, which is
determined less by the logic of syntax, as in the modern
system, than by rhetorical considerations affecting pronun-
ciation and the flow and rhythm of his sentences. For this
reason, the Riverside *Tom Jones* — though in modernizing
capitalization and spelling it concedes more to the expectations of the "general reader" than would be necessary in
Dr. Pangloss's world — will preserve, at least, the pointing
of the first edition. But the requirements of "popular" and
"definitive" editions are obviously distinct;[9] if some

8. Quotations from *Tom Jones* are from the Wesleyan edition, edd. M. C.
Battestin and Fredson Bowers (Middletown, Conn., and Oxford, 1974).
    9. Relevant to this distinction are the arguments by Arthur Brown and

compromises in the treatment of accidentals seemed
desirable for the Riverside *Tom Jones*, in the Wesleyan
edition Professor Bowers has carefully preserved all these
features of the original linguistic texture of the novel.

The *critical* necessity for such a procedure is clearly
demonstrable if one considers not merely the elementary
sense in which rhythm and emphasis are controlled by
pointing and capitalization, but the more dramatic ways in
which typographical variation (the use, especially, of italics
and different type sizes) may serve to signal an allusion or
otherwise to enrich the immediate context of a given
passage. In such instances the original accidentals of the
text must be respected not merely because they contribute
to the quaint flavor of the work (though a true con-
noisseur of eighteenth-century literature will wish to retain
them for that purpose alone), but because they have
acquired a substantive significance and can be tampered
with only at the sacrifice of understanding.

Let me illustrate, then, a few of the substantive uses of
typography in *Joseph Andrews* (1742) and *Tom Jones*
(1749), some relatively minor in importance, others quite
significant, but all affecting our experience of the novels.
To a reader familiar with twentieth-century typographical
conventions, the most obvious use to which Fielding puts
italics is to mark linguistic eccentricities in dialogue for
comic effect, as, for example, in the treatment of Squire
Western's broad Somersetshire accent:

'Come, my Lad,' says *Western*, *'D'off* thy *Quoat* and wash thy
*Feace*: For *att* in a devilish Pickle, I promise thee. Come,

John Russell Brown for and against old-spelling editions: see J. R. Brown's
"The Rationale of Old-Spelling Editions of the Plays of Shakespeare and His
Contemporaries," *Studies in Bibliography*, XIII (1960), 49-67, and the
rejoinder by Arthur Brown, *ibid.*, 69-76. Though this debate concerns the
somewhat different situation of Elizabethan and Jacobean dramatic texts,
most of the reasoning is applicable to works published during the earlier part
of the eighteenth century, at least. For reasons that will appear in the course
of the present essay, John Russell Brown's defense of partial modernization
seems to me cogent only with regard to "popular" editions, such as the
Riverside *Tom Jones*.

come, wash thyself, and *shat* go *Huome* with me; and *wel zee*
to *vind* thee another *Quoat*.' (V. xii, p. 265)

Similarly, the distinguishing *"Currycuristick"* (II. xiii,
p. 159)[10] of Mrs. Slipslop's speech — that "mighty Affecter
of hard Words" (I. iii, p. 26) — is the malapropism:

> 'Sure nothing can be a more simple *Contract* in a Woman,
> than to place her Affections on a Boy. . . . If we like a Man,
> the lightest Hint *sophisticates*. Whereas a Boy *proposes* upon
> us to break through all the *Regulations* of Modesty, before we
> can make any *Oppression* upon him. . . . Barbarous Monster!
> how have I deserved that my Passion should be *resulted* and
> treated with *Ironing*?' (I. vi, p. 33)

The same convention points up the lingo of hunters or
sharpers in *Tom Jones*, or the jargon of pettifoggers and
surgeons in *Joseph Andrews* — a notable instance being the
bawdy *double entendres* of the attorney in the stage-
coach, whose wit — cracked at Joseph's expense as
Fielding's hero endeavors to cover his nakedness with a
great coat — depends upon the terminology of real
property law:

> He said, 'if *Joseph* and the Lady were alone, he would be the
> more capable of making a *Conveyance* to her, as his Affairs
> were not *fettered* with any *Incumbrance*; he'd warrant, he
> soon suffered a *Recovery* by a Writ of *Entry*, which was the
> proper way to create *Heirs in Tail*; that for his own part, he
> would engage to make so *firm a Settlement* in a Coach, that
> there should be no Danger of an *Ejectment*;' . . . (I. xii, p. 54)

Word play of this sort is of course a delightful feature of
Fielding's comedy. What is more, as Glenn Hatfield has
shown,[11] it is part of a sustained satiric programme in his
writings calculated to reform and to purify the language;
for Fielding, like Locke, was troubled by the abuse of
words, the means of rational discourse among men and the
medium of his art. Considered in this light, such typo-

10. Unless otherwise noted, quotations from *Joseph Andrews* are from
the Wesleyan edition, ed. M. C. Battestin (Middletown, Conn., and Oxford,
1967).
11. *Henry Fielding and the Language of Irony* (Chicago, 1968).

graphical underscoring serves a useful substantive function.

Elsewhere, italics or other forms of typographical variation affect the reader's sense of context or heighten the humor of certain passages. In *Joseph Andrews*, for example, Fielding, who was a playwright before he was a novelist, sometimes uses italics within parentheses in an exchange of dialogue, imitating the convention for giving stage directions in printed plays:

> 'Consider, Child, (*laying her Hand carelessly upon his*) you are a handsome young Fellow, and might do better . . . .' (I. viii, p. 39)

> 'But the dear Man who is gone (*here she began to sob*) was he alive again, (*then she produced Tears*) could not upbraid me with any one Act of Tenderness or Passion.' (IV. vi, p. 297)

By this device, of course, Fielding underscores the artfulness behind Lady Booby's apparent spontaneities; he also, it seems to me, encourages the reader to visualize the scene as if it were taking place on stage. Or consider the effect of removing the italics from the following sentence in the Preface, where Fielding amusingly illustrates the impropriety of villainy as a subject for 'the Ridiculous':

> What could exceed the Absurdity of an Author, who should write the *Comedy of* Nero, *with the merry Incident of ripping up his Mother's Belly* . . . ? (p. 7)

By eliminating the italics here (as, until recently, every modern reprint has done), the editor may obscure for the reader the sense in which the entire phrase after "Nero" stands as the sub-title of the preposterous little drama Fielding has imagined (and which, incidentally, seems actually to have been performed as a droll at Bartholomew Fair![12]). A similar loss of specific point and humor results when the editor "romanizes" Parson Barnabas's advice to Adams on how to find a ready market for his sermons:

> 'I doubt that;' answered *Barnabas*: 'however, if you desire to

---

12. In *The Jacobite's Journal* (26 March 1748) Fielding refers to "the Conceit of a Fellow in *Bartholomew-Fair*, who exhibited the comical Humours of *Nero* ripping up his Mother's Belly. . . ."

make some Money of them, perhaps you may sell them by
advertising *the Manuscript Sermons of a Clergyman lately
deceased, all warranted Originals, and never printed.*' (I. xvi, p.
77)

For Fielding's first readers the phrase in italics was meant
to recall the "puffing" advertisements of certain booksellers, and very possibly of the notorious Thomas Osborne
in particular.[13]

In *Tom Jones*, furthermore, Fielding occasionally uses
typographical variation in quite remarkable ways to
*objectify*, as it were, the literary or moral qualities of
certain people he is satirizing. In the heading to the
introductory chapter of Book V, for example, he thus
archly alludes to John Rich's conception of pantomime, a
typical performance of which consisted of two parts
called "the Comic" and "the Serious": "*Of* THE
SERIOUS *in writing; and for what Purpose it is introduced*" (p. 209). The shift to roman upper case here does
more than merely supply emphasis; it embodies, typographically, the heaviness — "that superlative Degree of
Dulness," as Fielding puts it (p. 214) — which is the special
quality of Rich's entertainments. But the most striking and
delightful instance of this device in the novel occurs when
Fielding, ingeniously retaliating against those puny, slan-
derous critics who had condemned him for being "low,"
uses type actually as a visual emblem of his meaning:

> Such may likewise be suspected of deserving this Character,
> who without assigning any particular Faults, condemn the
> whole in general defamatory Terms; such as vile, dull, da—d
> Stuff, &c. and particularly by the Use of the Monosyllable
> Low; a Word which becomes the Mouth of no Critic who is not
> RIGHT HONOURABLE. (XI.i, p. 570)

The reduced font in which the words "Low, and "Critic"
are printed is the typographical equivalent of the *sense* of

13. Cf. Osborne's advertisment in *Common Sense* (13 and 20 December
1740): "*To be Dispos'd of,* / A Choice Collection of MANUSCRIPT SERMONS
of an eminent Divine lately deceas'd. In this Collection there is a Discourse for
every Sunday in the Year . . . which will be warranted Originals."

the adjective and the *meanness* or *pettiness* of the person, just as, to complete the jest and emphasize by contrast the triviality of Fielding's antagonists, the use of small capitals typographically approximates the idea of nobility and superior social station. Like Sterne after him, Fielding understood that at times the medium, the page of print, could be the message. Though he was not, of course, responsible in any general way for decisions concerning format, he was aware, as his editor must also be, that the reading of a book is a *visual* experience — that the arrangement of print and space, the choice of font and case, etc., create a visual texture that may even be exploited for iconographic effects.

The most frequent, and by far the most important, use of typographical variation in Fielding's novels is to signal an allusion, whether literary or topical. Surely, if he had had one of the original editons of *Joseph Andrews* before him, Professor Crane would have been better able to account for the pleasure he experienced, but coult not explain,[14] upon reading the following sentence describing the Captain's unhappy fate, whom Joseph has subdued with a chamberpot:

> The uplifted Hanger dropped from his Hand, and he fell prostrate on the Floor *with a lumpish Noise, and his Halfpence rattled in his Pocket*; . . . (III. ix, p. 258)

Fielding's italics here alert "the classical Reader" to the fact that he is parodying a formula that recurs in the *Iliad*: "He fell with a thud, and his armor clanged upon him." Similarly, without otherwise declaring the source of the allusion, Fielding in the following passages from *Tom Jones* uses italics to mark the echoes of some favorite poets that he has made a part of his own syntax:

> Reader . . . . Thou may'st remember *each bright* Churchill *of the Gallaxy* . . . . (IV. ii, p. 155, quoting Garth's *Dispensary* [1699], iv. 280.)

14. See "The Concept of Plot and the Plot of *Tom Jones*," in R. S. Crane, ed. *Critics and Criticism*, abridged edn. (Chicago, 1957), 91, n. 19.

[The conduct of parents forcing their children to marry unhappily] hath always appeared to me to be the most unaccountable of all the Absurdities, which ever entered into the Brain of *that strange prodigious Creature Man.* (VII. ix, p. 360, quoting Rochester's *Satyr against Mankind*.)

*Black George* was, in the main, a peaceable kind of Fellow, and nothing *choleric, nor rash*, yet did he bear about him some thing of what the Antients called the *Irascible*, and which his Wife, if she had been endowed with much *Wisdom, would have feared.* (IV. ix, p. 186, paraphrasing Hamlet's speech to Laertes, V. i.[15])

Some of the Company shed Tears at their Parting; and even the Philosopher *Square* wiped his Eyes, *albeit unused to the melting Mood.* As to Mrs. *Wilkins*, she dropt her Pearls as fast *as the Arabian Trees their Medicinal Gums*; ... (V. vii, p. 245, quoting *Othello*, V. ii).

It would be misleading, of course, to imply that the use of italics to mark an allusion in this way is an invariable feature of Fielding's texts. He is not consistent in the practice, sometimes using quotation marks instead and sometimes neglecting to provide any sort of signal. The device is, however, a frequent — and, as any of his commentators will attest, an important — means by which he tries to insure that the reader will not miss his intentions in a given passage.

In *Joseph Andrews* shifts of case or font serve as well to alert the reader to one of the novel's crucial thematic analogues, or to point the joke at Richardson's expense. Thus as Lady Booby, after the death of her husband, begins in earnest to hang out her lures for his hero, that paragon of chastity, Fielding writes: "she ordered *Joey*, whom for a good Reason we shall hereafter call JOSEPH, to bring up her Tea-kettle" (I. v, p. 29) — the use of small capitals here stressing the analogy between Joseph's character and situation and the biblical account of his namesake, who resisted the blandishments of Potiphar's wife (Genesis xxxix. 7-20). Similarly, the shift to italics

15. Fielding slightly alters the original: "For, though I am not splenitive and rash, Yet have I in me something dangerous, Which let thy wisdom fear."

for the last words of the novel — as Fielding assures the reader that his hero will not "be prevailed on by any Booksellers, or their Authors, to make his Appearance in *High-Life*" — underscores a facetious allusion to those spurious continuations of *Pamela*, *Pamela's Conduct in High Life* and *Pamela in High Life*, which had so irked Richardson that he was reluctantly moved to deliver his own authentic sequel.

Two further examples from *Joseph Andrews* are useful to illustrate the ways in which attentiveness to the accidentals of Fielding's text may lead to a fuller appreciation of his meaning. In the first, an unexpected irruption of capitals and italics very probably signals one of those private jokes that Fielding from time to time allowed himself for the entertainment of his closest friends. In relating to Adams the follies he had committed during his rake's progress through London, Mr. Wilson makes one confession that especially surprises the parson: to impress his acquaintance with his amatory conquests, Wilson had written love letters to himself, which, however, his friends knew to be counterfeit. Adams breaks in with an astonished exclamation:

> 'WRITE Letters to yourself!' said *Adams* staring!
> O Sir, answered the Gentleman, *It is the very Error of the Times*. (III.iii, p. 203)

It is tempting, at least, to suppose that the emphasis given to this exchange was calculated for the amusement of William Young, Fielding's good friend and the original of the absent-minded Parson Adams, who had achieved some temporary fame when, wishing to take a holiday from his duties as chaplain, he wrote a letter of invitation to himself, only to have the ruse discovered as he handed the letter, still sealed, to his patron.[16]

Finally, in my own limited experience as an editor the

---

16. For this amusing anecdote, see the account of Adams (dated 18 December 1742) quoted in the General Introduction to the Wesleyan edition of *Joseph Andrews*, p. xxii n.

most impressive proof of the soundess and practical efficacy of the Greg method is that its application to the text of *Joseph Andrews* resulted in the recovery of an important dimension, once entirely lost, of Fielding's satire. Until recently, no reader of *Joseph Andrews* had suspected that, like so many other characters in Fielding, Beau Didapper was drawn from a real-life original. From certain inconsistencies in Didapper's character, F. Homes Dudden thought it likely that some particular contemporary of Fielding's was being scored, but he could not say who it was.[17] The clue to the solution of the mystery was present all along in the accidentals of the original editions of the novel (and especially those of the *first* edition), where, curiously, running quotation marks are used to set off two passages in which Didapper's unprincipled politics and his vanity are described:[18]

> Now, to give him only a Dash or two on the affirmative Side:
> "Tho' he was born to an immense
> "Fortune, he chose, for the pitiful and dirty
> "Consideration of a Place of little consequence, to
> "depend entirely on the Will of a Fellow, whom they
> "call a Great-Man; who treated him with the utmost
> "Disrespect, and exacted of him a plenary Obedience
> "to his Commands; which he implicitly submitted to,
> "at the Expence of his Conscience, his Honour, and
> "of his Country; in which he had himself so very
> "large a Share." And to finish his Character, "As
> "he was entirely well satisfied with his own Person
> "and Parts, so he was very apt to ridicule and laugh
> "at any Imperfection in another." Such was the
> little Person or rather Thing that hopped after Lady
> *Booby* into Mr. *Adams's* Kitchin. (IV.ix, p. 313)

---

17. *Henry Fielding: His Life, Works and Times* (Oxford, 1952), I. 372.

18. The example neatly demonstrates the virtue of Greg's theory of copy-text: only in the first edition of *Joseph Andrews* do the quotation marks clearly enclose and separate the two passages in question. In subsequent editions the marks that closed the first passage and those that opened the second were eventually dropped, giving the false impression that Fielding had just one source in mind. In quoting, I have restored the running double quotation marks of the original to illustrate the form in which Fielding's first readers would have encountered this section of the narrative.

Presumably because this is not a passage of dialogue, every modern editor (since 1781) had removed the quotation marks, supposing some mistake of the compositor. (Another of the "discriminations of yesteryear" that would have amused John Crow.) Here, however, as in *Shamela* (1741),[19] Fielding's quotation marks signal that he is parodying, or in the second instance paraphrasing, passages from specific works: the first passage ironically inverts a compliment in Conyers Middleton's fulsome Dedication to John Lord Hervey in the *Life of Cicero*, where Middleton lauds Hervey's politics; the second passage echoes Pope's complaints in *A Letter to a Noble Lord*, where Hervey is ridiculed for his vanity and for his brutal sarcasm at the physical imperfections of others. Textual analysis having revealed the possibility of parody or paraphrase in these passages, once I had identified Fielding's sources other details linking the characters of Didapper and Hervey came to light easily.[20]

Like Pope, who has also preserved Hervey for us in the amber of *An Epistle to Dr. Arbuthnot*, Fielding was an author who, by a kind of creative alchemy, habitually transformed the particular and the idiosyncratic into the symbolic. Like Pope, he typically proceeds from the private reference to the universal implication. Unless the modern reader is kept aware of this fact — partly by the editor's supplying the commentary necessary to recover allusions and forgotten frames of reference, and partly, as we have seen, by his retaining the original typographical features of the text — significant dimensions of eighteenth-century works can be, and have been, lost. It is true, of course, that a modernizing editor may also retain, selectively, such typographical features of the original as appear to have substantive importance, but he runs a double

19. See the initial letter from Parson Tickletext to Parson Oliver, where the passages in quotation marks are parodies of the letters to the editor prefixed to the second edition of Richardson's *Pamela*.

20. For a full discussion of the evidence, see Battestin, "Lord Hervey's Role in *Joseph Andrews*," *Philological Quarterly*, XLII (1963), 226-41.

hazard in doing so: on the one hand, being fallible, he may not recognize the significance of the special case and so obliterate it; on the other hand, should he faithfully preserve them all, they will stand out, gauche and glaring, from the sophisticated texture in which he has clothed the work.

Having considered various topics for discussion on this occasion, I chose the substantive uses of accidentals chiefly because this was the aspect of Fielding's text that most fascinated me when I first seriously settled down to the business of editing his novels. My professional interests are essentially critical, not bibliographical, and it is as a critic that I have been most impressed with the usefulness of the Greg method in promoting the fullest possible appreciation of Fielding's art. Not only is the experience of reading Fielding's novels in a form that approximates their original "texture" qualitatively different from the experience of reading them in a modernized edition, but the effort to respect the accidental features of Fielding's texts has led in surprising ways to the recovery of his meaning in many particular passages. If this is "dogmatic systematization," as we have been told,[21] the dogma, being just and merciful, deserves its status as an article of faith in the true bibliographical church. I have not found, certainly, that the preservation of Fielding's original conventions of capitalization, spelling, pointing, and typographical variation presents, as we have also been told,[22] any real difficulties for the twentieth-century reader. For the reader who is likely to be interested in a "definitive" text of an eighteenth-century author, it has, moreover, its special pleasures and compensations.

Let me conclude, if I may, on a gratifying personal note that will be of general interest on this occasion. After being nine years in the making (something like this must be the period of gestation in Brobdingnag), the Wesleyan

---

21. See Greene, "No Dull Duty," p. 100.
22. See Greene, *ibid.*, p. 101, and *TLS*, 4 September 1969, p. 979.

edition of *Tom Jones* is due to see the light of day early
next year. Some of the problems that had to be solved
before the text could be established and the history of
composition and publication clarified were challenging
enough to have substituted as topics for this paper, but to
have rehearsed them in any detail would have been
supererogatory, as they are fully discussed in the introductions and notes to the edition. Since, however, our
conclusions with respect to the period of composition of
the novel and the relative authority of the first four
editions rather dramatically contradict accepted notions,
perhaps I might use the time remaining to me this evening
to summarize our findings and to suggest the reasoning and
the kinds of evidence that led to them.

The attempt at least roughly to determine the several
stages in the composition of the novel — to trace *Tom
Jones* as it evolved under Fielding's hand — naturally
required the weighing of all available evidence, both
external and internal, and the construction of the most
reasonable hypotheses that the evidence would allow. The
basic problem, and the most interesting, was of course the
fixing of a *terminus a quo* for a work which, by his own
admission, had cost Fielding "the Labours of some Years"
of his life.[23] For this purpose, external evidence was of
little use. From July 1744 — when Fielding publicly
disowned his Muse, declaring he had no intention of
writing any more fiction[24] — until June 1748 — when for
£600 he signed over to Andrew Millar the rights to *Tom
Jones* — only two references to the novel survive, both by
reliable witnesses but both, unfortunately, so belated that
their usefulness is negligible. What is more, they are so
cryptic in regard to Fielding's original intentions for the
novel that they raise more questions than they answer. The
earliest of these references occurs in that invaluable
bibliographical source, the ledgers of William Strahan, who

---

23. See Fielding's Dedication to Lyttelton, *Tom Jones*, p. 6.

24. See Fielding's Preface to the second edition of his sister's novel, *David
Simple*, published in July 1744.

in November 1747 recorded the printing of 250 "Receipts for M^r Fielding's Foundling";[25] the second appears in the correspondence of that avid literary gossip, Thomas Birch, who on 19 January 1748 informed Lord Orrery that "Mr. Fielding is printing three volumes of Adventures under the title of *The Foundling*."[26] What is one to make of these allusions to "Receipts" for *Tom Jones*, and to an edition of the novel in *three* volumes, half the number eventually published in February 1749. Did Fielding originally mean, as in the lucrative instance of the *Miscellanies*, to issue the novel by subscription, and in a much abridged form? For reasons too complex to enter into here, neither inference will bear scrutiny. It is more likely that Strahan's mention of "Receipts" implies an early scheme to issue the novel in two forms — one on fine paper, the other on coarse — and that Birch's reference to three volumes printing marks a stage in Fielding's execution of the plan for his great work when he was well enough satisfied with approximately half the manuscript to have considered submitting it to the printer. It is clear, at least, from Birch's remarks later in this same letter that Fielding had progressed far enough with the writing for Lyttelton to be able to commend the characterization and the conduct of the plot.[27]

Strahan and Birch are the only contemporary witnesses early enough to be of any help in fixing a *terminus a quo*, and, as we have seen, they are at least as mystifying as they are enlightening. This being the case, our only other source of information is the text itself. Fortunately, since *Tom Jones* is a highly topical book, it is potentially a rich source, but, as the experience of Fielding's biographers suggests, one more likely to delude than to reward the unwary. Piecing together clues supplied by topical allu-

25. B. M. Add. MSS. 48800.

26. See *The Orrery Papers*, ed. Countess of Cork and Orrery (London, 1903), II. 14.

27. "Mr. Littleton," Birch continued, "who has read the manuscript, commends the performance to me as an excellent one, and abounding with strong and lively painting of characters, and a very copious and happy invention in the conduct of the story."

sions in Fielding's narrative and in the prefatory essays that introduce each of the novel's eighteen books, Cross (and therefore Dudden, who follows Cross in all things) inferred that Fielding began *Tom Jones* shortly after June 1746, when, the Jacobite uprising having been suppressed, he discontinued *The True Patriot*.[28] At first glance, this seems a plausible hypothesis: the central narrative is, after all, set during the late autumn of 1745, when the Young Pretender was advancing toward the capital, and, among other datable allusions that might be cited, Books II and IV of the novel contain facetious references to John Freke's *Essay to Shew the Cause of Electricity*, published in October 1746.

But in their treatment of internal evidence Fielding's biographers were untroubled by a number of considerations that ought to have shaken their confidence in this line of speculation. For one thing — though topical allusions abound in *Tom Jones*, many of them to events that may be precisely dated — such allusions may safely provide a *terminus a quo* only for the particular passages in which they occur; they need not have been written at, or even very near, the time of the events to which they refer. Fielding, as is well known, habitually went over his manuscripts to enliven dull passages and to freshen those that had staled; indeed, the printer's records for *Tom Jones* reveal that he was tampering with his text even while the work was going through the press.[29] All one can safely conclude about a datable allusion in a work as extensive and as long in the making as *Tom Jones*, therefore, is that the allusion itself must postdate the event to which it refers; the chapter in which it appears may well have been written months, even years, earlier. With *Tom Jones*, furthermore, there is the special problem of the prolegomenous essays. By his own admission, Fielding could

28. See Wilbur L. Cross, *The History of Henry Fielding* (New Haven, 1918), II, 100 ff., and Dudden, II, 584 ff.

29. Strahan's entry for the first edition refers to "many Alterations," made presumably while the work was in press.

"with less Pains write one of the Books of this History,
than the Prefatory Chapter to each of them" (XVI. i);
rather than interrupt the flow of his narrative to compose
these essays, he quite probably reserved this chore for
some later time.

It sometimes happens, however, that the most telling
sort of internal evidence is the allusion that an author
*neglects* to make. If, as has been supposed, Fielding did
not begin *Tom Jones* until some time after June 1746, it is
puzzling that during the course of the first six books and
ten chapters of his narrative he nowhere alludes to the
rebellion; nor, with the single exception of an oblique
reference to the trial of the Jacobite lords (II, vi), does he
in the same space allude to any of the events associated
with the rebellion. This is true even though Fielding's
time-scheme requires that the action after Book V,
Chapter vi, be set in November 1745, "the very Time when
the late Rebellion was at the highest" (VII, xi). If Fielding
had this scheme in mind earlier, it is curious — especially
given his practice of interrupting his story at frequent
intervals to gossip with the reader — that he should have
avoided so scrupulously every opportunity of glancing at
an event which he regarded as the most critical in
England's recent history, an event "far more terrible to all
the Lovers of Liberty and the Protestant Religion, than
this Age had ever seen before, or is, I hope, in any Danger
of seeing again."[30] There are numerous early references to
the war with France, but, until the tenth Chapter of Book
VII, none at all to the rebellion. When, as late as the
second Chapter of Book VII, Jones seeks some meaningful
direction to give his life after his expulsion from Paradise
Hall, he can think of none, in despair choosing at last to go
to sea, not to defend his country against the rebels then, as
it appears, in full march toward London.

Contrary to Cross's deduction, what a consideration of
internal evidence in fact suggests is that when Fielding was

30. *The Jacobite's Journal* (13 August 1748).

composing the first six books (and more) of his narrative, he was unaware of the rebellion because it had not yet occurred. One may infer, then, that he had completed roughly one third of *Tom Jones* before August 1745, when news that Charles Edward had landed in Scotland first reached London. The plan of setting his central narrative in November 1745 was consequently an after-thought. Happily for this hypothesis, at least one sign that Fielding did alter an original chronology still survives in the text. In Book V, Chapter x, a point in the finished narrative just three weeks before that chill November day when Jones volunteers to march against the rebels, Fielding introduces his hero's amorous adventure with Molly Seagrim by observing: "It was now a pleasant Evening in the latter End of *June*." An error of five months in narrative chronology is not characteristic of Fielding, but the discrepancy is understandable according to the inter- pretation I would propose: that Fielding had progressed far into his novel by "the latter End of *June*" 1745; that he had completed another book and more of the narrative before news of the rebellion interrupted him in the late summer; and that, when he returned to *Tom Jones* after this most critical period in England's recent history had passed, he adjusted his original time-scheme so as to accommodate this event within the developing action of the novel.

The role played by internal evidence in fixing the period of composition for *Tom Jones* was therefore crucial, and in some respects surprising. The particular circumstances of the problem were, in fact, so unusual that the logic they required would not seem generally applicable. Though it is probably true in general that datable allusions in any long work that has been heavily revised should be treated warily — with greater caution, at least, than Fielding's biographers have shown — it would be rash to conclude from this one instance that what a novelist does *not* write is likely to be more useful in dating his work than what he does write. What is required to validate this method of deduction from omission is what obtained in the case of *Tom Jones*: a demonstrable *organic* connection between the finished work and the extrinsic historical event. As with *Tom Jones* and the "Forty Five," the event must be of such moment not only to the author but to the whole tenor and organization of his book that our suspicions are justifiably aroused when we cannot detect its influence where we would expect to find it. Lacking these conditions, an editor of *Roderick Random*, for example, would not wish to conclude that the first twenty-three chapters of that novel were written before the spring of 1741, the time of the calamitous battle at Carthagena that Smollett so vividly describes. An editor of *Tom Jones*, on the other hand, will be aware that after the rebellion of 1745 the threat of Jacobitism was a constant theme in Fielding's writings, just as the moment of the rebellion itself became the setting for his greatest work. It is not to be supposed that after August of 1745 he could have written two volumes and more of *Tom Jones* without more than a casual allusion to the subject, or without otherwise preparing the ground for the central movement of his narrative.

But if Fielding's biographers, and perhaps some of his critics, will be interested in the questions of when and how his masterpiece evolved, every serious reader will be concerned to know which of the four editions of *Tom Jones* published during Fielding's lifetime may be regarded as authoritative. Professor Bowers's solution to this essential problem departs radically from received opinion. I haven't the time at present — as I certainly haven't the temerity — to do more than summarize his arguments, which are of course fully set forth in the Textual Introduction to the Wesleyan edition. There, in a masterly — and, to his collaborator, an awesome — analysis of complex bibliographical evidence, Professor Bowers demonstrates conclusively that the fourth was the only edition to be revised by Fielding in any general way, and that it, rather than the third edition as Jensen argued,[31] alone represents Fielding's final intentions with regard to the substantives of the novel.[32] Though in his one and only revision of the third edition Fielding had extensively revised one sheet so as to intensify the attack on Jacobitism in the Man-of-the-Hill episode, it is now clear that in subjecting the fourth edition to a general revision, he *deliberately*, and at some considerable inconvenience to the compositor, restored this section of the novel to its original first-edition reading. Professor Bowers's solution to this fascinating bibliographical puzzle is among the splendid achievements of his career, for which Fielding's future readers will be grateful.

31. Gerard E. Jensen, "Proposals for a Definitive Edition of *Tom Jones*," *The Library*, 4th Ser., XVIII (December 1937), 314-30.

32. It is pleasant to note that, in preparing his own edition of *Tom Jones* for the Norton Critical Editions series, Sheridan Baker independently came to the conclusion, which Professor Bowers's reasoning demonstrates beyond all doubt, that the fourth edition is authoritative for the substantives. (See his edition [New York, 1973], pp. viii, 763-68.) Because it is based exclusively on the fourth edition, however, Professor Baker's text is flawed with respect to both accidentals and substantives. Except for the one sheet containing Fielding's revisions of the Man-of-the-Hill episode, the unauthoritative third edition served throughout as copy for the fourth; the fourth edition, therefore, with the exception of this one sheet, incorporates all the third-edition compositorial corruptions in both accidentals and substantives. Furthermore, even the fourth-edition resetting of the Man-of-the-Hill revision is imperfect. When the fourth-edition compositor came to this one third-edition sheet that Fielding had revised, he reverted, in this single instance, to the first edition for his copy; in so doing, he cancelled not only the political revisions of the third-edition sheet, as Fielding wished, but also those other incidental *literary* revisions which are clearly improvements. As Professor Bowers explains in the Textual Introduction to the Wesleyan edition, the critical editor of *Tom Jones* will follow the first edition for the accidentals, since it is closest to Fielding's manuscript, and he will incorporate into this text all those substantive revisions in subsequent editions which are demonstrably authorial. Though only the fourth edition has any *general* authority with respect to the substantives, yet, since one sheet of the third edition *was* revised by Fielding, the editor must decide which of these third-edition revisions Fielding meant to cancel and which he in all probability meant to retain.

# From Publishing to Editing
## *Gil Blas de Santillane:*
# An Evaluation of the Rival Claims
# of Practical and Ideal Editing

## Roger Laufer

Publishing *Gil Blas*

To proceed from publishing to editing may seem nonsense since a text has to be edited before it can be published. Yet, not quite so, in fact. Let me cite a personal experience.

I handed in the edited manuscript of Lesage's *Gil Blas de Santillane* to Editions Garnier at the beginning of October 1970. It still has not been sent to the printer.

Textual editing is a practical pursuit whose object is to give the public an opportunity to read a text that is either unavailable or available only in a poor edition. If the replacement is planned by the publisher of the previous edition, he waits for his stocks to have run out before he goes ahead. And that's the end of my story.

Editing is an applied art with communication for its aim. Analytical or Physical Bibliography has been challenged by editors and historians; purism, you know, is going out of fashion mainly because it imposes burdens completely out of proportion to results, and some bibliographical inferences have been proved to run counter to evidence from archives. Why rely on a form of archaeology

31

when written sources are extant? Neither can Physical Bibliography be pursued as a pure descriptive science, for a pure descriptive science does not exist. Any description is an abstraction and a construct which achieves purposefulness only if it answers its stated aim. Bibliographical description in its most sophisticated form compromises between the demands of book-collectors, historians, librarians and textual editors. Identification and description have been confused. Bibliography has ignored philology. This was a matter of fashion: textual bibliographers were the new editors and as such tended to over-state the importance of their approach. The time has come, it seems to me, for an evaluation of the rival claims of practical publishing and ideal editing.

Unless editing be merely an exercise in physical bibliography or in philology, it normally leads to publishing. Which means that a publisher has to be found and a market must exist. Publishing is commercial, whereas editing never is economically worthwhile. We lack university presses in France. A French publisher will therefore seek to make a direct or indirect profit, from the sale of a book or the prestige gained through subsidized specialist editing, a situation which holds true for all "reputable" publishing. In France, we have roughly two types of publishing houses: the large or medium-sized ones with an ever-increasing tendency towards concentration, and the small ones, one-man businesses combining as in bygone centuries book-selling and publishing. For the editor, the choice may be between freedom without guidance and an inadequate house-style.

I decided once that Montfaucon de Villars' *Le Comte de Gabalis*, a minor but influential and significant work from 1670, deserved to be re-published. I approached Nizet, a publisher-book-seller on the Place de la Sorbonne. He was prepared to publish anything provided funds were forthcoming. The University of Melbourne generously made money available, and some 1200 copies were printed in 1962. Many are still for sale, I assume, for Nizet never tells. He never publicizes, so that such a book does not reach the public. Perhaps, in the circumstances, that is a real service to the community, for a bad piece of editorship, thus, does no harm to scholarship. With a French education I had had no training in textual matters nor any knowledge of physical bibliography. A fac-simile reproduction of the 1670 text would have been a sensible solution; it was prevented by the size of the original duodecimo: 17 lines of text (98 x 58 mm) per page with roughly 25 characters per line. We decided to have it reset, keeping the old spelling and such peculiarities as long s'es and tildes, though not indicating the beginning of original lines or pages. We had 37 lines per page with some 56 characters per line; 76 pages as against 331, nearly one for five. Typeface, layout, format, paper distort the appearance and feel of the original: a mundane, airy pocket-book becomes a cramped pedantic block. Furthermore, the retaining of abbreviations (nasal tildes) used by the original type-setter to justify his lines (shortening them by an em or an en) becomes irrational and erratic when the lines are reset. Typography, punctuation and spelling are linked: they are Greg's "accidentals." I shall presently return to this basic problem.

In older texts, say sixteenth century, fac-simile offset reproduction has much to recommend it; reprinting has had the advantage of doing away with ill-conceived quasi diplomatic editing. In this connection, it has the same superiority as fac-simile title-page reproduction over quasi-fac-simile "reproduction" (both illegible and often erroneous). When a text has become inaccessible to the average educated reader, the more urgent skilled editorial task is to modernize or translate it.

We are, however, concerned with the eighteenth century. Though many phrases and words are apt to be misunderstood, the language and general allusions can still be understood with minor assistance. What are we then to do?

When I edited *Le Diable Boiteux* by Lesage in 1970, I

chose as copy-text the second revised edition of 1707, which came out only weeks after the first. The much altered and enlarged 1726 *Diable Boiteux* has been the standard version since its publication. Rightly or wrongly, I decided on literary grounds that the 1707 text is by far the better version. What about the critical apparatus and the accidentals?

The first edition contains few variants, except for a lengthy speech in the second last chapter, and presents no problem. The 1726 remake, on the other hand, is twice the size; expansion led to reshuffling. Lesage worked with scissors and glue. Though all displacements and cross-references are indicated in my apparatus, the numerous variants are hard to construe and, in practice, can only be used in a linear way, i.e., when the textual sequence remains more or less unchanged. Should not the editor's task in such a case be to select for publication a number of variants while writing a full-length critical study of his comparative material? The practice imposed on Balzac editors by Editions Garnier for commercial reasons, although it is too restricted, makes perhaps better sense than an erudite apparatus that will probably never be used consistently by anyone. My main purpose in editing *Le Diable Boiteux* was to give a preliminary essay on physical aspects of the second edition. Mouton published, the book as a piece of pure research. The absence of a commercial publisher's judgment on the text proper may again have been detrimental and resulted in the publication of material unfit for human consumption.

This concerns the substantive readings of authoritative versions of one novel rewritten to the extent that Lesage may have created two separate works. What about accidentals?

Some historical considerations will clarify matters. At the beginning of the eighteenth century, variant spellings were still numerous though limited to the use of single or double consonants, . accents or consonants (es/é in particular in a closed syllable or in the last syllable, the

ending of the second person plural és/ez, etc.), presence or
absence of the acute on a non-final open syllable
(medecin/médecin), choice of final y or i (icy/ici), z or s.
By the middle 1720's, spelling had become more regular,
and in the thirties the modern norms had been established
with very few differences. Punctuation followed
approximately the same pattern, though rules remained
ill-defined.

In the 1707 *Diable Boiteux*, I was able to identify the
work of two type-setters through various means, among
them their preference for final i or y. I made a special
study of capitals, discovered a few rules which account for
some apparent inconsistencies, yet found that they were
applied only occasionally and were semantically redundant
except in one instance where the use of the capital
distinguishes the noun from the adjective. Jean Fabre
assures us that Rousseau discriminated in his manuscript
on the *Gouvernement de Pologne* between such words as
*Peuple* and *peuple, Souverain* and *souverain*, etc.[1] I for one
have not been able to discover the nuance and, from my
own experience, suggest that at most a capital is a mark of
nobility and dignity, and, more or less as in modern
French usage, distinguishes between *Etat* français and *état*
d'esprit, and so on. An editor's job is not to reproduce
literally an author's manuscript when it exists unless he
can prove that idiosyncracies carry a special meaning. The
Pléiade edition of Rousseau, admirable as it is in many
respects, is merely pedantic in insisting on Rousseau's own
spelling. The onus should be on the editor, not on the
reader. I am sure I was right in deciding to modernize
spelling and capitalization while retaining variants which
indicate that a word had a different currency: thus, har*a*m
instead of har*e*m, but c*ou*vent and not c*on*vent (a then
normal spelling which looks unnecessarily odd to us).

On punctuation, however, I must confess that I have
changed. In *Le Diable Boiteux* I retained the old original

1. J. J. Rousseau, *OEuvres Complètes*, t. III, ccxliv.

punctuation; in *Gil Blas* I have modernized it. This was the
publisher's wish and my choice.

To put the matter in its proper perspective, allow me to
quote Walter Greg's definition:

> We need to draw a distinction between the significant, or as I
> shall call them 'substantive' readings of the text, those namely
> that affect the author's meaning or the essence of his
> expression, and others, such in general as spelling,
> punctuation, word-division, and the like, affecting mainly its
> formal presentation, which may be regarded as the accidents,
> or as I shall call them 'accidentals' of the text.[2]

This distinction was used to justify the theory of a double
authority for substantives and accidentals, recently refined
by Fredson Bowers.[3] For accidentals, we follow the
original edition or manuscript, or attempt to reconstruct
it; for substantives, we generally follow the last
authoritative edition,[4] embodying the author's revision.

Let us read Greg's text closely. It seems nicely balanced
through its use of opposing words and clauses, such as "or
as I shall call them 'substantive' readings of the text" and
"or as I shall call them 'accidentals' of the text." The
distinction he draws is based on the scholastic opposition
between substance and accident, essence and form.
Substance is identified with essence, accident with form.
The scholastic argument, however, turns out to be a mere
rhetorical device used to hide Greg's fundamental assertion
that meaning and authority are substantial and not
accidental. Greg's silence is the more important part of his
statement, for he has nothing to say on the relationship
between accidentals and meaning or authority. The
dichotomy between "author's meaning" and *printer's form*
remains latent. Greg even avoids to parallel the phrase

2. "The Rationale of Copy-Text," *Studies in Bibliography*, III (1950-51),
19-36.

3. Fredson Bowers, "Multiple Authority: New Problems and Concepts of
Copy-Text," *Library* (1972).

4. I have dealt in general terms with the question of authority in my
*Introduction à la Textologie* (Paris: Larousse, 1972), 18-23; concerning *Gil
Blas*, see below pp. 39-44.

"substantive" readings with *accidental readings*. For this simple phrase would upset his whole construct: an accidental reading may have a meaning which is not the author's. De Saussure's classic distinction between *le signifiant* and *le signifié*[5] reminds us that Greg's substantives and accidentals both belong to the *signifiant*, and cannot constitute operative classes, which indeed should not surprise physical bibliographers.

Greg's theory comes really to saying that accidentals are so trivial that an author hardly ever bothers to revise them while emending words or sentences, but, nevertheless, the original accidentals should be preserved at all costs. I'll grant that some authors insist on their own accidentals so that unwanted alterations should be done away with. However, in the vast majority of cases it is not so. As a result, the editor's *accidentalness* is sheer pedantry, and the theory is self-contradictory. Why bother about the insignificant? Are all accidentals insignificant? Obviously not. Greg's classes beg the question.

Substantives are words or sets of words, that is, sequences of letters. Changes in letters may or may not alter meaning, that depends on the period and context. To consider spelling variants as accidentals implies a particular philosophy of the standard language, which gained currency through the eighteenth century and became established in the nineteenth. Yet, in spite of various efforts, it never was possible fully to standardize punctuation, let alone fonts, sizes, lay-out, etc. The problem is that texts are reproduced by the use of a notational system (the alphabet and numbers), a semi-notational system (the punctuation signs), and loosely expressive means (the typographic style). An edition is not only the reproduction of a text according to a notational system (i.e., old- versus new-spelling) but a unique performance[6] of the text. With the growing impact of visual media, the distinction drawn

5. *Cours de Linguistique générale* (Paris, Payot, 2e ed.), 97-100, 155-162.
6. These distinctions are based on Nelson Goodman's *Language of Art* (Bobbs-Merrill, 1968).

by Greg has become less and less acceptable. In fact, publishers have always had to be style-conscious. A text reads as it looks. Editing should also be a visual art.

Must everything be modernized? No. An eighteenth century text bears indelible marks of its day and age. I have mentioned word currency. This may apply to notions: it is normal to extend our use of capitals to those that then would have called for them and thus distinguish between *Ciel* and *ciel, Cour* and *cour*, etc. As regards punctuation, the use of hyphens, dashes or paragraphs to introduce direct speech is to be proscribed because a purely linguistic notation was used (*dire, répondre, repartir, ajouter, poursuivre*, etc.): the two systems are not compatible. Yet, as a rule, punctilious editors have paid no attention to this matter and left it to the printers.

I have followed modern usage in generalizing the use of an exclamation mark after *Ah*'s and *Oh*'s while sometimes retaining the distinctive usage of semi-colons and colons in long sentences, a usage which has gone out for stylistic reasons but can be readily grasped in context. Commas are more tricky; the single comma between a clause qualifying the subject and the main verb has become unacceptable. It looks wrong. If the subject is a noun, we have to introduce an additional comma before the clause; if it is a pronoun, we must strike out the single comma. Very frequently an infinitive clause was preceded by a comma; this is still possible but gives a special emphasis which should not be read into the older text. As a rule, I have struck out such commas.

What I have attempted to do is to handle separately but consistently each type of problem, in order to make the text accessible not only to the common reader but also to the specialist of a different period. I grant that my edition will not be definitive and only hope that it may one day be contemporary. This is not so sad, for once the distinction between accidentals and substantives is dropped, as it must be, the concept of a definitive edition loses its cogency. Doubtless when an editor brings together the original accidentals and the final substantives of a text, he creates a definitive edition. Greg's theory gives a scientific alibi for this demiurgic activity. If we reject the theory's claim to general validity, while admitting its empirical value in many instances, we must recognize that Fredson Bowers' more recent practice, conservative as it is in recommending old spelling, is only one form of eclecticism, based on a biographical understanding of textual history. The editor has two choices: either he strictly reproduces the unique performance[7] of his basic text and puts all variants in his critical apparatus (thus putting the onus on the reader), or he produces, according to a set of rules which he must lay down, one of several possible eclectic performances. The situation is one we are familiar with as regards annotation: either we do not help the reader on the grounds that contemporaries needed no assistance, or else we explain allusions, words, esthetic effects, etc., according to what we feel but cannot prove is most needed, and the amount of space at our disposal.

The theory of the double authority of substantives and accidentals is tenable but not definitive.

Accidentals, though, may be of great value to the editor in proportion to their insignificance. In the same way as the precise position of signatures shows at one glance whether two printed copies with similar line-by-line setting belong to the same edition or not, accidentals may be the quickest means of finding out how editions are derived, at any rate up to the time when punctuation ceases to fluctuate. Had I realized this earlier, I should have saved time and labour in establishing the true derivation of authorized (i.e., duly licensed) editions of *Gil Blas de Santillane* published during Lesage's lifetime. A little know-how is often worth much bookish knowledge. Is physical bibliography more for the editor than a set of tips? And that makes it invaluable, as we should remember when we turn from publishing to editing.

7. This unique performance may comprise multiple states and variants.

Editing *Gil Blas*

*Gil Blas*, with *Don Quixote* and *Robinson Crusoe*, was one of the most widely read and influential novels throughout the eighteenth and nineteenth centuries. It has been published some 250 times in French, and its text has naturally deteriorated. It originally came out over a period of twenty years: two volumes in 1715, one more in 1724, and one more again in 1735. In 1747, posthumously perhaps, a complete revised edition was issued. That edition, though inconsistent in matters of spelling and punctuation, became the basic copy-text from the 1820 Neufchâteau edition onward. Dupouy gave a fairly accurate edition of the 1747 text in 1935 and Etiemble in 1960 a critical edition with variants based on the so-called "1732-1737 edition."

Roughly speaking, we have to choose between two versions: the one that follows the text as it was published over the years, the other that embodies the author's final revisions. In view of the time-gap (thirty-two years between Vol. I-II and Vol. IV), it is not surprising that Lesage, attempting to unify his novel in order to leave a testamentary version of it, indeed did not enter into the original spirit of the work and imposed an extraneous and only partial coherence on the work. Tomashevski's principle of the unitary creative mood[8] suggests that the 1747 version should not be chosen as copy-text. Etiemble was mistaken, however, in trusting the advice of a librarian-bibliographer[9] who had recommended the so-called 1732-1737 edition. The truth of the matter is that there is no such edition: there is a 1732 edition of the first three volumes and a title-page cancel dated 1737, designed to match the 1732 title-page, for the unsold copies of the second 1735 edition of the fourth and final

---

8. Boris Tomashevski, *Pisatel' i Kniga. Očerk tekstologii* (Priboj, Leningrad, 1928), 164.
9. J. Calemard, "Une erreur littéraire à propos de *Gil Blas*," *Bulletin du Bibliophile et du Bibliothécaire* (1926), 350-364, 405-418.

volume. Thus the 1732-1737 Bibliothèque Nationale set belongs to a re-issue and not a separate edition of the work. It remains nonetheless true that a number of minor authorial revisions distinguish the re-issue from a bibliophile's set of original 1715, 1724 and 1735 copies.

How can the puzzle be solved? The 1737 fourth volume re-issue gives us a clue: there must exist a missing link between the 1735 original and the 1737 cancel since 1737 and 1735 belong to different editions. 1737 is indeed a re-issue of a second edition published in 1735 as proved by several copies with the cancellans title-page bearing the imprint 1735. The revised fourth volume belongs to the silent second edition. For the first two volumes, second editions, with the fact acknowledged on the title-page, were published in the same year as the original: these contain all the authorial variants which seemed to lend some authority to the two first volumes published in 1732. What about the third volume?

The original title page (on a conjunct leaf) of the 1724 book bears the surprising statement "Edition nouvelle." A variant title-page has been described by Cordier.[10] Though I have not been able to locate a complete copy without the mention, I happen to own a disbound made-up copy with the variant title-page as a loose leaf. Comparison shows that, apart from the added statement and the consequent lowering of the ornament on the page, the setting is identical, and the last line bears the same spelling mistake "Appobation" for "Approbation." We may induce, from these facts, that the puzzling mention is the result of a stop-press alteration decided upon for commercial reasons. The intermediary 1729 edition does not contain any of the 1732 variants, though part of it was used as copy-text in 1732. We must conclude that the third volume of the 1732 edition constitutes a second revised edition. This is not unlikely, since Lesage was probably then working on the

10. Henri Cordier, *Essai bibliographique sur les Œuvres d'Alain-René Lesage* (1910), 77.

fourth and final volume: he would have corrected his copy
of the third volume in the process.

Which text should be selected for a critical edition?

For volumes I, II and IV, there is no choice but to
accept the second editions, dated the same year as the
original and probably printed a few months later. Indeed,
it may be considered that, in the first half of the
eighteenth century (and no doubt this would apply to
earlier and later times), second editions give the finally
revised text (something like our corrected page-proofs) and
not a subsequent revision of it. Volume III, however,
embodies corrections that were made some eight years
after the original publication. Although not numerous and
obviously hasty (many errors were left unchanged), they
must be assigned to the author, as will be seen:

| 1724 | 1732 |
|---|---|
| je me montrai fort sensible à *ses bontés* | *volontés* |
| pour *capter*[11] ma bienveillance | *captiver* |
| Que de talents! vous *avez,* pour me servir d'une expression de | Que de talents vous *réunissez en vous! ou plutôt*, pour me servir d'une expression de |
| notre tripot, vous avez l'outil universel. | |
| Mon coffre-fort, m'écriais-je, mes chères richesses, qu'êtes-vous devenues? | Mon coffre-fort, m'écriais-je, *où êtes-vous?* mes chères richesses? qu'êtes-vous devenues? |
| la victoire que je *remporte des* seigneurs | que je *vais remporter de mes chers* seigneurs |

Most of these variants display the trends already present in
the 1726 *Diable Boiteux* variants and later carried to
extremes in the 1747 revised *Gil Blas*: expansion and
academicism. On Tomashevski's principle of greatest inner

11. In the contemporary edition of Richelet's *Dictionnaire de la langue
française ancienne et moderne* (1728), *capter* is daggered as low, whereas
*captiver* is the acceptable word.

cohesion, I therefore decide on their rejection. Yet, the fourth volume was published only three years subsequently. Is it not closer in style to the rejected variants? In view of the changes in tone noticeable in both 1724 and 1735, this does not seem to be a valid literary argument. Lesage failed to unify the three instalments of his major novel, and this failure accounts for both its shortcomings and achievements. Rather, I must insist on the different nature of second edition variants (1715 and 1735), limited as they are to minor emendations or corrections.[12]

I have therefore chosen as copy-text for each volume respectively $1715^2$, $1715^2$, 1724, and $1735^2$, while of course emending the text with $1715^1$ and $1735^1$. The 1732 variants as well as the abundant 1747 ones have been relegated to the critical apparatus. Nevertheless, if only for this purpose, it was necessary to study the derivation of the various editions. The stemma for each volume is as follows:

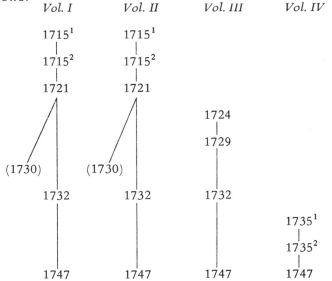

12. The first two volumes of 1732 may each contain three or four very minor authorial corrections.

All editions are linearly descended, except that the first two volumes of the 1729-1730 edition are collaterals. This one surprising exception may be explained by the fact that it combines 1715[1] and 1715[2]: the hybrid had a prolific descent which can be traced down to the 1947 Bardon edition published by Garnier. It is worth noting that the first two volumes bear the correct notations on the title-page "Seconde Edition," "Troisième Edition" and "Quatrième Edition" from 1715[2] to 1732.

The stemma is clearly established by the "substantive" variants on pp. 45-46.

It appears from the stemma that the 1730 variants of volumes I and II should not appear in the critical apparatus, since they do not belong to the authorized tradition. Instead of collating the variants as has to be done with manuscripts, I could have used the evidence from accidentals and saved days of unnecessary work. 1721, 1730 and 1732 are typographically related, but 1732 follows 1721 more closely, and even line by line. Whereas 1730 and 1732 tend to modernize spelling (for example, *eût* for 1721 *eust*), punctuation links 1721 and 1732. A sampling of punctuation and line-setting would have been enough to prove that 1730 is a collateral branch.

The 1729 (or 1730 with new title-page) variants of volume III on the contrary belong to the tradition. 1724, 1729 and 1732 are typographically very close, and a study of accidentals does not show any immediate difference. This, in itself, is subsidiary evidence of close relationship.

Misprints result in accidental or substantive errors, according to Greg's terminology. Here again, I suggest that the distinction is misleading. Two words run together may give rise to an unnecessary authorial emendation: *pour compenser* → *pourcompenser* → *pour récompenser*; *qu'il l'avait* → *qu'il avait* → *qu'il le tenait*. A dropped or poorly inked letter is interpreted as a transposition: *de [b]ons enfants* → *de nos enfants*. A lower-case l, misused for an exclamation mark, suggests that the punctuation mark has been omitted and the l should be capitalized: *Comment*

## Vol. I

| 1715¹ | 1715² | 1721 | 1729-30 | 1732 | 1747 |
|---|---|---|---|---|---|
| *femme de chambre* | petite bourgeoise | petite bourgeoise | petite bourgeoise *femme de chambre* | petite bourgeoise | petite bourgeoise petite bourgeoise |
| [1715¹ cancellans] | [1715¹ cancel] | | | | |
| *m'écriai-je* | dis-je | dis-je | *m'écriai-je* | dis-je | dis-je |
| de quoi occuper | de quoi occuper | de quoi *vouloir* occuper | de quoi occuper | de quoi *vouloir* occuper | de quoi occuper |
| dans un âge avancé | dans un âge avancé | dans un âge avancé | dans un âge avancé | d'un âge avancé | d'un âge avancé |
| m'obligeait à | m'obligeait à | m'obligeait à | m'obligeait à | m'obligeait de | m'obligeait de |

## Vol. II

| 1715¹ | 1715² | 1721 | 1729-30 | 1732 | 1747 |
|---|---|---|---|---|---|
| *princesse* | dame | dame | dame | dame | dame |
| *dame* | personne | personne | personne | personne | personne |
| rentra | rentra | rentra | *entra* | rentra | rentra |
| ressouvenir | ressouvenir | ressouvenir | *souvenir* | ressouvenir | ressouvenir |
| encore là payer | encore là payer | encore *la* payer | encore *la* payer | encore *la* payer | encore payer |
| il y avait | il y avait | il y avait | il y avait | *elle* avait | *elle* avait |
| originale | originale | originale | originale | *parfaite* | *parfaite* |

## Vol. III

| 1724 | 1729 | 1732 | 1747 |
|---|---|---|---|
| *frisait* | faisait | faisait | faisait |
| bontés | bontés | *volontés* | *marques d'affection* |
| repenti *et* enfin | repenti enfin | repenti enfin | repenti enfin |
| *qu'il l'avait* | qu'il avait | qu'il avait | *qu'il le tenait* |

## Vol. IV

| 1735[1] | 1735[2] | 1747 |
|---|---|---|
| contre Kermès | contre le kermès | contre le kermès |
| tout argent | tout l'argent | tout l'argent |
| et fis | et je fis | et je fis |
| dites-lui qu'il | dites-lui qu'il | je vous ordonne de lui dire qu'il |

*vous appelle-t-on, mon ami l On m'appelle → mon ami?
L'on m'appelle.* An author's correction is generally inferior
to his original phrasing, which shows how true
Tomashevski's view is.

Lesage is no exception to the rule. Furthermore, he is
often prompted by the error to enlarge on his original
text:

| 1721 | 1732 | 1747 |
|------|------|------|
| consumé | *consommé* | consumé à eux seuls |
| quatre éditions | | |
| je hais la coquetterie, *et* | je hais la coquetterie, | je hais la coquetterie: ce que les hommes ne sauraient assez payer, |
| je suis une tourterelle pour la fidélité. | | |

| 1729 | 1732 | 1747 |
|------|------|------|
| qu'il s'enrichirait | qu'il s'enrichissait | qu'il s'enrichirait infailliblement |
| quand même il serait honnête homme. | | |

Such variants are not different in nature from the
hundreds of minor additions that characterize the 1747
revised version and so weigh it down. Nonetheless, we have
every reason to suspect that in such instances as the above
sheer typographic errors have catalyzed the fatal process.

Had I chosen to edit the 1747 text, I should have had to
decide whether or not to incorporate in the text the
variants prompted by typographical mistakes, and would
have been inevitably wrong. My problem was limited to
the apparatus, which admits of an easier solution: to give
the intermediary misprint and the final emendation. The
reader can form his own opinion.

The publisher agreed to print the slightly expanded
apparatus. He refused, however, my request to use
different marks in the body of the text to refer to original
and later variants. He also persuaded me to rewrite one

sentence in the introduction in which I stated that Etiemble's 1960 text had been my editing copy. The objection was commercial though not very well taken, it seems to me. I am pleased to be able to state clearly here my indebtedness because of its editorial significance.

For nothing is perfect, even with publishing, and editors, on an occasion such as this, may be allowed to take comfort from each other.

# On Annotating *Clarissa*

# John Carroll

My first minor bout with problems of editing eighteenth-century novels came in 1957. As part of an oral examination for the doctorate, I was asked to explicate a passage of my choosing from the literature of the Augustan period. I chose Book IV, chapter vi of *Tom Jones* because it seemed to me a passage in which Fielding faced up to important problems about Tom's moral nature – and also dodged certain problems. Well before the examination, I had martialled passages from *Tom Jones* and other works by Fielding as well as passages from such luminaries as Bishop Butler and Lord Shaftesbury to explain the novelist's assumptions and assertions about morality. But one detail eluded me. Fielding compared the moral monitor in Tom's breast to the "famous trunk-maker in the Playhouse."

This phrase bothered me not only because I had no idea of who the trunk-maker was but because I was certain all of my examiners *would* know and that they would pounce on this allusion as one of the keys to the whole passage. The adjective "famous" suggested to me that anyone who professed a knowledge of the eighteenth century could not fail to be acquainted with this fellow. In a mild panic, I wrote to Professor James A. Work, who, I understood, was editing *Tom Jones.* Who was the trunk-maker in the playhouse? A post-card immediately came back from Professor Work to this effect: "I have no idea. But if you find out, please let me know." The reply was heartening — if he didn't know, who did? — and so, armed with his profession of ignorance, I entered the examination. No one asked me about the famous trunk-maker.

A few months later, I was reading through the *Spectator* when I found the answer to the problem. In *Spectator* 235, Joseph Addison observes "that of late years there has been a certain person in the upper gallery of the playhouse, who when he is pleased with any thing that is acted upon the stage, expresses his approbation by a loud knock upon the benches or the wainscot, which may be heard over the whole theatre." Because the blows resembled those given in the shops of trunk-makers, this self-appointed critic was given his name. Like the Lord Chancellor, to whom Fielding also compares the inner voice of morality, the trunk-maker was incorruptible. He never laid on his blows for a bad play. Well, there you have the explanation. In the afterglow of serendipity, I simultaneously dispatched the information to Professor Work and to *Notes and Queries.*[1]

The moral of this anecdote is, in some ways, not really a moral lesson at all. In finding sources, we are partially at the mercy of blind luck. On the other hand, the luck often consists in knowing what problems are to be solved. Without Book IV, chapter vi of *Tom Jones* in mind, who would take second thought of the trunk-maker in Addison's essay? In Addison's hands, the reference seems to be clearly to a contemporary character, well-known to the audiences of the time; in Fielding's passage, the reference is no longer to a character immediately familiar to his audience but to one who, presumably, would be familiar

---

1. John Carroll, "Fielding and the 'Trunk-maker,'" *N&Q*, June 1959.

only through the *Spectator* essay. Yet Fielding refers to him as "famous" and makes the reference as though anyone would instantly grasp it. Perhaps many members of his contemporary audience would understand the allusion at first glance. To the twentieth-century editor, however, not to say the common reader of our times, such allusions are teasing reminders of how ignorant we are of the common currency of a former age. Such as Fielding and Richardson are shall Fitzgerald and Hemingway be.

To counterbalance the tale of my success in tracing the trunk-maker to his perch in the theatre, I would like to refer to my problems with a difficult passage in *Clarissa*. After a pyrotechnical burst of rhetoric justifying his treatment of Clarissa, Lovelace writes to his friend Belford, "Thou wilt call this a prettiness or A WHITE BEAR!"[2] Now, the meaning of the passage is quite clear. Lovelace has made the worse appear the better cause, the black (or dark brown) appear white. But why the phrase "A WHITE BEAR"? The allusion is tossed in as casually as the reference to the trunk-maker, but it is put in capital letters. In some ways, it seems that while Richardson is calling attention to the phrase by the type, he expects his audience to seize upon it as a familiar phrase. I have searched in vain for a totally adequate answer to the origin of this allusion. Indeed I have plagued colleagues with the problem so often that they probably began saying to themselves, "Exit the editor, pursuing a bear."

Pliny mentions that all bears are born white and then are licked into shape and darkness by their mothers. In the first act of *The Old Wives Tale*, the old man says to the two brothers, "If any ask who told you this good,/ Say the white bear of England's wood." When I asked the latest editor of this play for an explanation, the reply was that the passage remains a crux. To leap over the centuries, Walter Shandy uses the white bear to great rhetorical effect when he is working on the Tristrapaedia. But

2. Samuel Richardson, *Clarissa* (1748), VII, 29.

Obadiah Walker, who was Sterne's source for this decla-
mation on the power of auxiliary verbs, does not summon
up white bears to make his point.[3] Whence the white bear?
The closest I have come to answering the question is a
proverb attributed to Jacques Yver in the sixteenth
century: "His eloquence can serve to make the crowe seem
white."[4] There you have the essence of the matter; it can
be explained in terms of black-white imagery, of a proverb,
but the *bear* is still missing. The explanation is — and
should be — enough to satisfy the ordinary reader, but to
the editor, and to those scholars looking over his shoulder,
the quintessential explanation is missing.

As for the trunk-maker, the meaning of the allusion is
also quite clear in the context; nevertheless, one wants to
know more, particularly whether the allusion gives a twist
to the passage that we may not be aware of. Perhaps it is at
this point that one turns from remarks about serendipity
and lost white bears to the psychology of the editor. The
eighteenth-century novel provides a vast editorial terrain.
Anyone who edits a novel, particularly of this period, must
be tempted to look on the editor of a play as blessed. I
should think that the best motivations·for anyone editing
the very long texts of Fielding and Richardson and
Smollett must be unquenchable admiration and sheer
curiosity, the kind of curiosity that keeps one searching
even after an allusion has been relatively well explained.

I undertook the editing of *Clarissa* not only because of
my admiration for the novel but because I was very
curious indeed about what the annotations would show
concerning Richardson's reading, his general knowledge.
Richardson's education has always been something of a
mystery. T.C.D. Eaves and Ben Kimpel have suggested that
he *might* have attended the Merchant Taylor's school for a
time, but that remains a possibility, not a certainty.[5] In a

3. Laurence Sterne, *Tristram Shandy*, Volume V, chapter xliii.
4. Jacques Yver, *A Courtlie Controversie of Cupids Cantles* (1578),
quoted in the *Oxford Dictionary of English Proverbs*.
5. T.C.D. Eaves and Ben Kimpel, *Samuel Richardson* (Oxford, 1971) pp.
9-10.

letter written in 1753, he said that his father designed him for the ministry, but, because of heavy financial losses, Richardson Sr. could not give him the needed education. "He left me to choose at the Age of 15 or 16, a Business; having been able to give me only common School-Learning: I chose that of a Printer, tho' a Stranger to it, as what I thought would gratify my Thirst after Reading."[6] Richardson then says that he stole from his own hours of rest and relaxation his reading times, even buying his own candles so that his master was cheated neither of time nor of tallow.

From his letters, actually, one can derive a good deal of information about his reading. Richardson comments, for example, that he read Ariosto in his younger days, at a time when he had more faith in romance than he had afterwards, and that he wished for Angelica's invisible ring.[7] When denouncing Charlotte Lennox's *Shakespeare Illustrated*, he wrote of Shakespeare, "I will for ever revere Thee, for what I have read, and, many Years ago, seen acted of thine, and hope to live to read the rest of Thee, the far greater Part; which has been postponed as the Reformation of the Roman Governor of Judea was in hopes of a more convenient Season than yet I have found."[8] Yet he was to say later that although Shakespeare was a greater author than Addison, he was inferior to Addison as a man because "in his best writings, *less useful.*"[9] He praises the imagination and invention of Spenser in exclamatory terms, but confesses that "for want of time, or opportunity, I have not read his Fairy Queen through in series, or at a heat, as I may call it."[10] (I think Richardson may be forgiven on that score, for I have never known anyone who read *The Faerie Queene* through at a heat!) He refers to Milton as "glorious," calls Dryden's

6. *Selected Letters of Samuel Richardson*, ed. John Carroll (Oxford, 1964), p. 229.
   7. *Ibid.*, p. 235.
   8. *Ibid.*, p. 250.
   9. *Ibid.*, p. 335.
   10. *Ibid.*, p. 162.

comedies "licentious and wretched," has little good to say about Pope and Swift.[11] What emerges from this necessarily brief survey is that even with regard to the authors he praises most highly — Shakespeare and Spenser — there are indications that he was not familiar with the entirety of their works. Perhaps the whole matter is best summarized in a line from Richardson to Aaron Hill in 1743: "I seldom read but as a Printer, having so much of that and a Head so little able to bear it."[12]

One intriguing question, then, was what the annotated *Clarissa* might prove further about his literary background. Of course, there was the other intriguing question of what changes he made in the text over the years, but since I have discussed this aspect of the edition elsewhere,[13] I shall restrict myself here to the "explanatory notes." Over the years, many critics have talked in general or specific terms about his possible indebtedness to drama. In *Samuel Richardson and the Dramatic Novel*, for example, Ira Konigsberg endeavours to track down Richardson's debt to the stage of the Restoration and eighteenth century. I thought at the time I read this study that it was more successful in suggesting parallels than in finding specific indebtedness, and after working on *Clarissa* I think that judgment the correct one. R. A. Day's *Told in Letters: Epistolary Fiction before Richardson* is based on a reading of over 200 epistolary novels between the Restoration and 1740. But Day concludes that although Richardson's techniques and themes had certainly appeared in this form prior to *Pamela*, one cannot say that Richardson specifically owed anything to this body of work. The self-made, self-educated Richardson would certainly have nodded his approval of the conclusion that he was free of any kind of debt.

It should, of course, be remarked that Richardson

11. *Ibid.*, pp. 176, 334, 56-8, 213-15.
12. *Ibid.*, p. 59.
13. John Carroll, "Richardson at Work," *Studies in the Eighteenth Century I*, ed. R. F. Brissenden (Canberra, 1973), pp. 53-71.

thought of himself as, in his own words, creating a new species of writing in *Pamela*. Indeed, one of the constant refrains in the letters is his freedom from all but his own experience and imagination. Nevertheless, his novels are studded with a great many quotations from and allusions to English, continental, and classical literature. Richardson's attitude toward the use of direct quotation is partially explained in a letter to Miss Elizabeth Carter. Miss Carter had been upset because he used her "Ode to Wisdom" in the first edition of the novel without her permission. Let me say in defence of Richardson that he didn't obtain the permission simply because he was unaware of who the author was. In a letter of apology to her, after she had taken him to task, Richardson said that he did "not want Matter" for the piece he had then ready for the press, that he indeed had a redundance of it, and had parted with several beautiful transcripts from the best poets to shorten the novel. He went on to say that he had inserted the quotations to "enliven" a work which was perhaps too solemn.[14]

Now that word *enliven* presents some difficulties. From one angle, it seems to imply that his transcripts of beauties are ornamental, or, to vary the metaphor, oases, in a prose work of over 2000 pages. On the other hand, that word does not rule out a functional use. A quotation or an allusion might well be used to further the significance of a passage, to intensify its significance by reference to the words of another character, another author, commenting on a parallel situation.

Since my edition is the first one to attempt a full annotation of *Clarissa*, I feel free to introduce some statistics by way of news — or at least by way of communicating some unknown facts. In *Clarissa* there are 106 quotations from or allusions to English poets and dramatists. The sources of three of these have still eluded me. The 103 I have identified come to a great extent from

14. Eaves and Kimpel, pp. 214-16.

the literature of the Restoration and early eighteenth century. Despite what Richardson says of Dryden's comedies, he is easily the most quoted of the authors. There are also quotations from twenty-five other writers of this period, including Lee, Cowley, Milton, Rowe, Prior, Pope, Norriss, Congreve, Waller, Hill, and so on. The great exception to my statement about chronology is the use of Shakespearean material. Shakespeare, with twelve quotations, is second only to Dryden.

Even after identifying these quotations, and placing them in statistical order, one is still not in a position to say that Richardson was quoting from what he had read. As A. D. McKillop and A. Dwight Culler pointed out several years ago, Richardson seems to have used Edward Bysshe's *Art of English Poetry*, and possibly Charles Gildon's *Thesaurus Dramaticus* as resources for many of these quotations. Forty-three passages quoted by Richardson may be found in Bysshe's collection of beauties from English drama and poetry. When Richardson wanted a quotation in a passage about despair or madness or rape or women, he could reach over to the shelf, take down Bysshe, and find what he needed. Up to a point, these parallels between Bysshe and Richardson might seem to be mere chance. But when one finds two quotations in the same passage in *Clarissa* and on the same page of Bysshe, or finds both misquoting in exactly the same way, the editor is reminded of Thoreau's comment on circumstantial evidence.

A great many of the other passages are so well known that he need not have had a profound knowledge of the original to produce them when the occasion seemed warranted. Among the allusions, however, are a few that puzzle one because the sources seem so remote from anything Richardson would be likely to have known.

In the opening volume, Clarissa comments on vain and conceited girls who must see the decline of the summer's sun and the onset of the winter of age.[15] There is, by the

15. *Clarissa*, I, 276.

way, no direct indication here that Richardson is recalling Clarissa in *The Rape of the Lock*. Yet Richardson's very choice of the name Clarissa might raise some wonder as to whether he was, in some way, affected by Pope's use of the name for the cool, rational, moralizing antithesis of Belinda. In *The Rape of the Lock*, many of the sentiments of this reasoning voice might well be those of Richardson's Clarissa, but there is of course one element possessed by Pope's character denied to Richardson's. Pope gives his spokesman a sense of humour, a gloss of wordly-wise irony. In any event, Richardson's heroine goes on to say that these girls will be like another Helen, who "will be unable to bear the reflection even of her own glass." This is obviously an aspect of the legend of Helen that is not readily remembered by the ordinary reader — nor by the ordinary editor. The passage is, however, explained by reference to Thomas Heywood's *The Iron Age*, Part II, where Helen asks Hermione for a mirror and says:

> Where is that beauty, liues it in this face
> Which hath set two parts of the World at warre . . .
> I am growne old, and Death is ages due . . .
> *She strangles herselfe.*[16]

Now this is a perfect illustration of the legend of Helen which the novelist is using here. But is Thomas Heywood the source? It is possible, yet somehow one feels that the same scene, described in a different context, by another author might well be Richardson's source. Certainly, he nowhere else refers to Thomas Heywood, and yet, of course the literary historian might find it very appropriate indeed that Richardson knew Thomas Heywood's work.

Or, to take another example, late in the novel Lovelace's friend Belford refers to a "Whining Tom Essence," in the context of discussing how eighteenth century dramatists are incapable of creating real distress. Now Tom Essence is the hero of Thomas Rawlins's *Tom Essence; or the Modish Wife*, which had only one edition, in 1676. Tom is a

---

16. Thomas Heywood, *The Iron Age*, *Works* (London, 1874), III, 429-30.

cowardly city man who dreads being cuckolded. In one
typical scene he says, "I'le drown myself in tears, and lay
my death to his [the betrayer's] charge: oh, oh, oh (cry)".
For very good reasons, Rawlins's play was not a staple of
the 18th century stage, yet Richardson introduces the
hero's name as though it were as familiar as that, say, of
Belvidera. Perhaps the name had become a by-word for a
foolish, tear-besotted man; perhaps it was in common
currency; on the other hand, I recall no other reference to
this character in works of Richardson's contemporaries. To
move to some allusions that do not raise such questions
about the knowledgeability Richardson expected from his
audience, there is a reference to the story of Herod and
Mariamne, a story that would be familiar through the
*Spectator* and Elijah Fenton's play. Richardson does not
refer specifically to Josephus's *History of Jewish Anti-
quities* as his source but the novelist knew Josephus, for
Lovelace in another allusion, refers to the passage where
Hazael strangled Adad with a wet cloth. Lovelace says that
perhaps the cloth was dampened with laudanum, and
thereby Richardson suggests, before the rape, that Lovelace has such a possibility in mind for Clarissa.

Many of these quotations or allusions are, so to speak,
imbedded in the text — not set off as separate quotations.
Early in the novel, Lovelace arouses Clarissa's jealousy by
seeming to be enamoured of the daughter of an inn-keeper
whom he calls Rosebud. Anna Howe is the conveyor of the
news and relates his praise of Rosebud's "wild note" as a
singer. In the next letter, Clarissa picks up this phrase and
comments scornfully on the way Rosebud "warbles
prettily her wild notes."[17] The allusion to "L'Allegro" is
unmistakeable, and, interestingly, Richardson does not
throw the phrase in gratuitously but prepares for the
allusion and weaves it neatly and unobtrusively into
Clarissa's letter. In another passage of the second volume,
Clarissa writes, "*Pride* and *Meanness* I have often thought,

17. *Clarissa*, II, 148.

are as nearly ally'd, and as close borderers upon each
other, as the poet tells us *Wit* and *Madness* are."[18] Here,
the allusion to *Absalom and Achitophel* is quite clear,
though again not identified by Richardson, and one might
add it is not used for mere decoration but to bolster
Clarissa's acute point about the thin boundaries between
Pride and Meanness, a point borne in on her hourly by the
actions of her family.

The casual quotation is often, too, a means of charac-
terizing the person introducing it. Lovelace refers in
passing to lines in Prior about doubling down the pages of
the Bible at useful places. This allusion is to "Hans
Carvel," one of Prior's bawdiest poems — and, therefore,
one concludes after finding the source, an example of a
poem that would stick in the rake's mind. The poem is not
quoted by Bysshe or any other anthologist whom I have
examined; so it is a poem which apparently lingered in
Richardson's mind as well. And to refer to still another
typical allusion, Lovelace says to Belford, "Thou remem-
berest the Host's tale in Ariosto. And *thy* experience, as
well as mine, can furnish out twenty Fiamettas in proof of
the imbecility of the sex."[19] Now this story is one in which
Jocundo finds his wife unfaithful, and, in his cynicism,
decides with a friend to take their pleasure of all women in
their travels. Finally, they agree to share one mistress, who
despite their precaution of making her sleep between
them, still manages to be unfaithful. The story fits very
well indeed into Lovelace's previous view that no woman is
of impregnable virtue. Yet now, of course, he has
encountered the one woman who disproves that idea.

One of the more interesting allusions that characterizes
Lovelace is that in which he suggests he is of Montaigne's
taste, who "thought it a glory to subdue a girl of family.
More truly delightful to me the seduction progress than
the crowning act — For that's a vapour, a bubble."[20] This

18. *Ibid.*, II, 305. cf. *Absalom and Achitophel*, 11. 163-4.
19. *Clarissa*, V, 273.
20. *Ibid.*, IV, 94.

is the hero at his self-revelatory best; the perverseness of
his imagination is summed up here, but by the allusion,
Lovelace indicates that he is not alone in having such
tastes. The relevant passage is in Montaigne's essay entitled
"Of Three Commerces or Societies":

> I have coveted to set an edge on that sensuall pleasure by
> difficultie, by desire, and for some glory. And liked Tiberius
> his fashions, who in his amours was swaied as much by
> modesty and noblenesse as by any other quality ... Surely
> glittering pearles and silken cloathes adde some-thing unto it,
> and so doe titles, nobilities, and a worthie traine. Besides
> which, I made high esteeme of the minde, yet so as the body
> might not justly be found fault withall.[21]

It is also in keeping with Lovelace's character that
Montaigne should compare himself to a Roman emperor, a
matter to which I shall turn later.

What these selected passages show, in microcosm, is that
some authors had written lines or phrases that were a part
of Richardson's memory. They do not show that Richardson was "influenced" by any of them in such a way that
they shaped his art or his conception of human experience
as the result of having absorbed them. And yet one cannot
help dwelling on the multiplicity of references to Dryden
and Shakespeare. Both Dryden's poetry and his tragedies
often seem to be Lovelace's proper mode of expression
when he reaches for an appropriate quotation: the heroic
conception of self in Dryden's dramas, the largeness of the
claims on the imagination, suit Lovelace. And perhaps it is
significant, when one recalls that Richardson's characters
are described as being always of "divided mind", that four
of the Shakespearean quotations come from *Hamlet*.

Of the works referred to directly by Richardson, one
that functions very interestingly indeed in the novel is
*Venice Preserved*. After they arrive in London, Lovelace
takes Clarissa to a production of the play. He is sure at this
stage of the action, that by watching this drama she will be
"softened." Considering certain aspects of the play, one

21. *The Essays of Montaigne*, tr. John Florio (New York, 1933), p. 744.

sees how appropriate it is that this is the one theatrical
performance Clarissa attends in the city. We are hardly
more than a few moments into the play when Belvidera's
father says to Jaffeir:

> You stole her frome me! Like a thief you stole her,
> At dead of night; that cursed hour you chose
> To rifle me of all my heart held dear,
> May all your joys in her prove false like mine
> A sterile fortune and a barren bed
> Attend you both; continued discord make
> Your days and nights bitter and grievous still
> May the hard hand of a vexatious need
> Oppress and grind you, till at last you find
> The curse of disobedience all your portion.

At this time Clarissa suffers most heavily in her mind from
the curse that her father places on her both in this world
and the next, and thus the impact of that speech on her
would be only too clear. Just as clear after the tragedy was
acted would be the moral of the couplet with which
Belvidera's father ends the play:

> Spare no tears when you this tale relate,
> But bid all cruel fathers dread my fate.

His burden of sorrow at the end should suggest to Clarissa
that her own father may have to — as he in fact does —
express similar sentiments.

There is another aspect of the play that might well have
appealed to Lovelace's perverse mind. It surely would have
pleased one of his mentality to see Clarissa, who actually
goes to the play from Mrs. Sinclair's brothel, view with
abhorence the actions of the prostitute Aqulina. Clarissa
lived in the very milieu that would have seemed so
repellent to her on the stage.

To turn from the profane to the holy, the single work
most often quoted is the Bible. There are 93 references to
the Old and New Testament and seven to Apochrypha.
Thirty seven of these references are to the Book of Job.
After the rape, Clarissa, as you will recall, writes her so
called "Meditations," and most of these "Meditations" —

either direct quotations or verses slightly altered to suit her position — are based on that book. The quotations are appropriate for very obvious reasons; Clarissa, to Richardson, was a latter-day Job, one who underwent inexplicable sufferings. The frequency of references to the Bible emphasizes the point that Richardson said he most wanted to make. In discussing the wishes of those who wanted a happy ending, Richardson wrote "The History, or rather, the Dramatic Narrative of *Clarissa*, is founded on a Religious plan."[22]

The quotations from the Bible establish, too, the groundwork of Clarissa's education. Were it not for her religious nature, formed by Dr. Lewen and Mrs. Norton through the Bible, she would not have the strength, the fortitude, that she does. The novel turns around Clarissa's refusal to abdicate her will, to acknowledge the sovereignty of Lovelace. Their battle is not only between sexes, between classes, but also between the diabolical and the heavenly. Clarissa and Lovelace are role-players with strong imaginations. They take their conflict seriously; they realize that they are shaping each other's destinies. Clarissa's loss of her physical virginity becomes equivalent in her own mind — and that of Lovelace — to the destruction of an empire. Objectively, this is not true, but it *is* true in the minds and hearts of the chief characters. Through the frequent references to the Bible, the characters remind us that the drama is played on a cosmic stage and involves the salvation of one soul and the destruction of another. The Biblical quotations and allusions function, in short, in a way that the verses of Dryden and his contemporaries do not.

In the conclusion, which as Richardson says, is "supposed to be written by Mr. Belford," the tone that Clarissa has imparted to the narrative by her frequent quotations from the Bible influenced Belford himself, the rake who becomes a different man by his bearing witness to the

22. *Clarissa*, VII, 426.

dying Clarissa. Alluding to Zechariah, he refers to himself as a "brand plucked from the fire." The phrase is familiar to everyone, but its total appropriateness is evident only when one remembers the whole passage:

> And he shewed me Joshua the high priest standing before the angel of the Lord, and Satan standing at his right hand to resist him.
>
> And the Lord said unto Satan, the Lord Rebuke thee, O Satan: even the Lord that hath chosen Jerusalem rebuke thee: is not this a brand plucked out of the fire?
>
> Now Joshua was clothed with filthy garments, and stood before the angel.
>
> And he answered and spake unto those that stood before him, saying, Take away the filthy garments from him. And unto him he said, Behold, I have caused thine iniquity to pass from thee, and I will clothe thee with change of raiment.[23]

The context of the Biblical passage, then, is a reminder, as Richardson says in various sections of all his novels, that reformation comes only through God's grace, and here, obviously, Belford, the boon companion of Lovelace in the old carefree days, puts off his filthy garments. Satan is present at this moment just as he is present at the beginning of the Book of Job. Throughout the work, Lovelace has been identified with the devil — both by himself and by Clarissa. As Satan could not subdue Job, so Lovelace cannot conquer Clarissa; and, despite Lovelace's self-proclaimed superiority to the awkward and gauche Belford, it is his graceless friend who has put on new garments by the end of the novel.

Richardson could, of course, depend on the Biblical phrase, the long Biblical quotation to strike an echo in the breast of every reader. The extent of the reverberations of those echoes — whether one connected, say, The Book of Job and Zechariah — might be another matter. But in two other areas, he could well depend on a widespread knowledge of the sources of his allusion. There are eight

23. Zechariah, 3, 1-4.

references to Aesop, to such stories as the contest of the sun and the wind, to the tale of the jay with borrowed plumage.

For Richardson, such references would readily leap to his mind because he had revised Sir Roger L'Estrange's edition of Aesop and published it in 1739. These references are made primarily by Lovelace, who uses them to express, in his mad way, a common-sensical view of what he is doing in his pursuit of Clarissa. Lovelace justifies himself then, not only by summoning up Dryden or Nat. Rowe, but by referring to the kind of shrewdness that is Aesop's stock in trade.

As Lovelace uses Aesop to explain or justify what he is doing, so Lord M. uses proverbs to admonish his nephew against expending his spirit — and money — in a waste of shame. Lord M. is a retired rake himself, and his typical mode of expression leads one to think of him as a kind of aristocratic Sancho Panza. He has a proverb for every occasion. After tracing many of Richardson's quotations to Bysshe, I thought that there might well be a collection which Richardson used to give Lord M. the maxims with which he sprinkles his conversation. In fact, I found nearly all of them in the 1678 collection of John Ray's proverbs. As Lord M. uses these proverbs, they appear, to Lovelace as the maunderings of one who now mumbles the game he dare not bite. The use of a proverb is equivalent to a nervous tic for Lord M., and Lovelace so regards it. The hero rejects the shopworn wisdom of the generations for a liberated, contemptuous mode of his own expression — or for the ironies of Aesop.

The last point I want to touch upon concerns Richardson's use of language. Lovelace prides himself on his freedom with words; it is equivalent to his tearing off the shackles of Christian morals. Spotting unusual use of words in the 1740s is partially a matter of guess work. Perhaps I have missed some unusual usages, but I have found that, according to the *OED*, Richardson was the first to introduce 10 words on the printed page in *Clarissa*;

he uses seven words that are recorded for the last time in the *OED*; two phrases are not recorded at all. Although I have not checked this point I suspect that the record of first, last, and only usages is higher in *Pamela*. But nevertheless, even this record of unusual usages in *Clarissa* reflects Richardson's own freedom from the expectations an eighteenth-century audience might have of a "correct" style.

It would be possible to dwell at great length on Richardson's allusions to history and to mythology. The comparisons of Lovelace to Tiresias and Proteus are especially revealing. Lovelace is so successful with women because he can enter their minds (the mind of every woman, that is, except Clarissa) and because he can assume so many shapes, so many roles. His allusions to Caesar, Hannibal, and Alexander remind us that he is in the tradition of the "great man" in eighteenth-century literature, one who prefers power over others to goodness in himself. Before the rape, Lovelace introduces historical parallels to magnify his campaign; after the rape, the generals and emperors are introduced to minimize what he has done.

I have in this paper presented a survey of the terrain, and have tried to suggest points of particular interest as well as recurrent characteristics of the landscape. Not only Bysshe and Ray but many of Richardson's friends who read the novel in manuscript, such as Aaron Hill and Edward Young, may have suggested quotations, allusions, parallels. In our present state of knowledge about Richardson, even a reference to *A Midsummer Night's Dream* cannot be ascribed to his memory.

As I have already suggested, the last quotation has not been identified. Shortly before Clarissa's death, Lovelace refers to her as one

   — whose mind
contains a world, and seems for all things fram'd.

Though there is a line and a half of poetry, which might

come from any number of sources, it reminds one of *Paradise Lost* (VIII, 473 ff.) where Adam speaks of seeing Eve for the first time:

> That what seemed fair in all the World, seemed now
> Mean, or in her summed up, in her contained.

The parallel is there, and Richardson does change quotations to suit his purposes, but is this really an adequate reference? The question must be left to time — other readers, other editors.

The disconsolate editor, faced with the last seemingly insoluble problems and worried by possible errors as his material goes to the press may, of course, take solace from Samuel Johnson, who says of editors, "sudden fits of inadvertency will surprise vigilance, slight avocations will seduce attention, and casual eclipses of the mind will darken learning; the writer shall often in vain trace his memory at the moment of need, for that which yesterday he knew with intuitive readiness, and which will come uncalled into his thoughts tomorrow."[24] And yet few of us are in a state where we can dismiss our work with "frigid tranquility."

I think it is evident that Richardson, like Fielding, was not merely writing for the young, the ignorant, and the idle. The range of his allusions and quotations suggest that he had sophisticated readers such as Samuel Johnson in mind as well as the naive, would-be goddess or the naive, would-be Don Juan. Indeed, *Clarissa* is pervaded by a sense that human life is played out against a background of time-past, recorded in literature, and against the background of all eternity, foreshadowed in the Bible. In the last analysis, it is not his knowledge of what had been written, but his understanding of what the human being is, in all his contradictoriness, that makes Richardson the bearer of light into the recesses of the human mind.

24. Samuel Johnson, 'Preface,' *Dictionary of the English Language* (1785).

# The Sterne Edition:
# The Text of *Tristram Shandy*

## Melvyn New

Sooner or later – and probably within the first year of
assuming the title – the general editor of a scholarly
edition of a major author is bound to ask himself
plaintively, "why me?" Setting aside for the moment the
hopes of glory and immortality fostered by attaching
myself to Laurence Sterne, the answer for me lies in a
critical assumption about the works of Sterne: that he was
a satirist and that the meaning of a work like *Tristram
Shandy* will best be illustrated by a thoroughly annotated
edition, along the lines of Guthkelch and Smith's *Tale of a
Tub* or Kerby-Miller's *Martinus Scriblerus*. But one cannot
annotate a text before establishing it, and one cannot
establish a text before collating numerous texts, and one
cannot collate before understanding something about
bibliography. The path is a familiar one to all of you, I am
sure; but I would like to stress that I began – and
eventually hope to end – with a conviction that what I
was doing would help to explain what Sterne was doing;
that is, I began as, and hope to remain, a student of the
words of the book and not of the book itself.

I introduce myself to you in this manner because I am

frankly intimidated by the fact that my interest in annotating *Tristram Shandy* has brought me, by routes reminiscent of Tristram's diagrams of his own progress, before an audience of bibliographical experts. Indeed, had this conference been called, as it might have been, a "conference on the science of editing," I am not sure I could have found the courage to face you; I do feel more at home, however, at a conference on editorial problems, for what I have discovered above all else in the past few years as general editor for Sterne's *Works* (and more specifically, as textual editor for *Tristram*) is that editing is a problematic endeavor from beginning to end. We all remember Uncle Toby's response to the astonishment of Dr. Slop that babies could be born without "scientific operators"; and I may well paraphrase him, "I wish you had seen what prodigious editions we had on library shelves before Greg and Bowers." Like Walter, I have kept company with the good doctors in my study below, but the real work of delivering the edition of Sterne, it seems to me, will have to be done by the midwife upstairs. Today I would like to put before you some of the many problems of the Sterne edition and a few tentative solutions for them. I would also like to impart to you my conviction that the practice and procedures of editing a text are determined at all crucial points by the nature of the canon and the particular work being edited – and, might I add, by the personal choices and critical judgments which everywhere govern the working editor.

We may begin with the canon of Sterne as I found it when the project first got underway in 1969. The letters of Sterne had been brilliantly edited thirty-four years earlier by Lewis Perry Curtis,[1] and there appeared to be no reason to redo what he had done so well. The few letters that have turned up since will be published in a volume of *Miscellanies*, along with a new edition of Sterne's "Memoirs" and the "Journal to Eliza," both of which Curtis

---

1. (Oxford: Oxford University Press, 1935).

included but which can profitably be re-edited. The volume of *Miscellanies* will also include *A Political Romance*, Sterne's first sustained creative work, which has recently appeared in Ian Jack's Oxford English Novels edition, and in a facsimile edition for the Scolar Press.[2] A well annotated edition of this satiric allegory is still highly desirable, however, and an understanding of the work will be greatly enhanced by the publication with it of the three pamphlets which preceded the *Romance*. A small textual problem has also appeared since Jack's edition, due to the discovery of a variant state (among the six surviving copies) by Edward Simmen.[3] Other miscellaneous works of Sterne include early newspaper writing, some of which involves problems of attribution; his poem, "The Unknown World," printed first in the *Gentleman's Magazine* in 1743 and years later, supposedly from manuscript, by Thomas Gill;[4] the Stapfer fragment, that rather mysterious dream-fantasy about worlds upon worlds, which first appeared in Paul Stapfer's 1870 biography of Sterne, with a story of its discovery that might well turn a bibliographer's hair gray;[5] and, finally, the Rabelaisian fragment, which first appeared in a bowdlerized version in Lydia Medalle's 1775 collection of her father's letters, and which I recently re-edited from the Pierpont Morgan Library holograph.[6] In short, the *Miscellanies*, as might be

2. *A Sentimental Journey with The Journal to Eliza and A Political Romance* (Oxford: Oxford University Press, 1968); *A Political Romance* (Menston, England: Scolar Press, 1971). An annotated edition of the *Romance* was prepared by G. W. Donnelly as a Master's thesis under my direction, University of Florida, 1970.

3. "Sterne's *A Political Romance*: New Light from a Printer's Copy," *Papers of the Bibliographical Society of America*, 64 (1970), 419-29.

4. *Vallis Eboracensis* (London and Easingwold, 1852), 198-200. See Wilbur Cross, *The Life and Times of Laurence Sterne*, Third Edition (New Haven: Yale University Press, 1929), 597.

5. *Laurence Sterne — Sa Personne et ses Ouvrages — Étude précédée d'un Fragment inédit de Sterne* (Paris: Ernest Thorin, 1870), xvi-xlix. Stapfer tells the story in his introduction of how he received the holograph of the "Fragment Inédit" from a friend of a friend, copied and returned it, and was never able to view it again (pp. xi-xii).

6. *PMLA*, 87 (1972), 1083-92.

expected, will confront their editor with the full range of editorial problems, from attribution and variant texts on the one hand, to historical and analytical annotation on the other.

In 1967 Gardner D. Stout published his edition of *A Sentimental Journey*,[7] a fine example of the editing we hope to achieve for the rest of Sterne's canon, and it is our hopeful expectation that Professor Stout will provide a second edition of the *Journey* for the *Works*. Even here, however, one begins to be aware of the truly problematic nature of editing, for objections have been raised because Stout, in spite of his enormous diligence in establishing his text, did not take into account the very large number of accidental variants of the second edition, published eleven days after the death of Sterne; Stout had collated the first and second editions and had decided the second had no textual importance.[8] My own complaint against Stout's edition — and I hope it is not mere carping — is that his annotation, while magnificent in its fullness in most instances, is rather slanted towards his critical view of the *Journey* as a compromise between satire and sentiment; hence he is somewhat incomplete in his commentary on Sterne's bawdy undercurrents, which I would suggest need ample annotation to prevent Sterne's point from being lost.[9] This is not to say, however, that Stout's edition is inadequate, either textually or in the notes, for it is not. Rather, Stout's edition demonstrates that one truth all editors must eventually discover, and which Samuel Johnson, whose wisdom shaped his editing, but who perhaps also became wiser for the editing that he did, stated so beautifully: "He that has abilities to conceive perfection, will not easily be content without it; and since perfection cannot be reached, will lose the opportunity of

7. (Berkeley and Los Angeles: University of California Press, 1967).

8. Stout, p. 319. The objection was raised in *TLS*, December 12, 1968, p. 1410.

9. The same point has been made by Ronald Paulson in his review of Stout, *Journal of English and Germanic Philology*, 67 (1968), 712-13.

doing well in the vain hope of unattainable excellence."[10]

Sterne's sermons were published in four volumes during his lifetime and in three additional volumes a year after his death, forty-five sermons in all. Two sermons were published much earlier than the collected editions, one in 1747 ("The Case of Elijah and the Widow of Zerephath, considered"), and one in 1750, "The Abuses of Conscience," which, of course, also appears in *Tristram Shandy*; copies of both have survived. And at least two sermons survive in manuscript versions, "Penances" in the Pierpont Morgan Library, and "The Temporal Advantages of Religion" in the Huntington. To add to the editorial problem, the first two volumes of sermons, published in 1760, went through four editions that year and five more editions before Sterne's death in 1768.[11] In modern times, the sermons have appeared in their entirety only in the standard editions of 1904 and 1927, although Douglas Grant included a commendable selection of them in his edition of Sterne's works for the Reynard Press.[12] Quite clearly, this is one area in which a modern edition is absolutely required, particularly in view of the increasing importance some critics are giving to Sterne's religious views. The problems of annotating the sermons have been amply adumbrated in Lansing V. Hammond's *Laurence Sterne's Sermons of Mr Yorick*,[13] which attempts to locate the sources of Sterne's quite free pilferings; the extent to which such borrowings ought to be traced is perhaps not the least of the problems involved.

We come, then, to Sterne's greatest work, *The Life and Opinions of Tristram Shandy, Gentleman*, which has, to be

10. *Rambler*, no. 134; *The Rambler*, ed. W. J. Bate and A. B. Strauss (New Haven: Yale University Press, 1969), IV, 349.

11. Cross, pp. 600-601, 619-21; two additional sermons in manuscript listed by Cross have not yet been located.

12. *Sterne* (Cambridge, Mass.: Harvard University Press, 1970). Professor Grant had agreed to serve as one of the advisory editors for the present edition before his sudden death in 1969. A selection of the sermons, edited by Marjorie David, has been announced for publication in late 1973 by the Carcanet Press (Fyfield Books).

13. (New Haven: Yale University Press, 1948).

sure, been edited many times in the twentieth century. James A. Work's textbook edition (1940)[14] is still the best; its annotations are admirably suited to its function (though a few errors have turned up in the course of preparing the present edition), and its text is acceptably accurate. I should be well satisfied indeed if my fellow editors and I can do what we believe ought to be done for *Tristram* as well as Professor Work did what he wanted to do. What we believe ought to be done, and the problems encountered in doing it, must be our next concern.

The nine volumes of *Tristram Shandy* were published in sets of two, with a single last volume, by three different publishers over an eight year period, 1760-1767; no manuscripts have survived. The complicated history of these early editions has been recently unraveled by Kenneth Monkman, whose work — and advice — have proved invaluable in establishing the bibliographical under-pinnings for the present edition.[15] Two years of sub-sequent investigations, and machine collation, have added very little to his findings — and what has been added is of minimal significance.

Mr. Monkman has succeeded in establishing the textual importance of the first edition of Volumes I and II, which appeared in late December, 1759, or January, 1760, with no imprint save the date, and which, he has now clearly demonstrated, was printed in York by Ann Ward some three or four months before Robert Dodsley published the first London edition. This second edition was used as the copy text by Work and by Ian Watt in his 1965 Riverside edition. The present edition will use the York text, for it seems quite certain that it was set from Sterne's manu-script, Sterne having failed in his initial attempt to interest

14. (New York: Odyssey Press, 1940).
15. "The Bibliography of the Early Editions of *Tristram Shandy*," *Library*, 25 (1970), 11-39. The present essay may be seen as supplemental to Monkman's; I tried to avoid the simple repetition of his basic findings and concentrated on those few areas where collation and further investigation have turned up additional information.

Dodsley in the work. In some ways, perhaps, the York printing is as close as we will ever get to Sterne's manuscript of *Tristram*. Surely Dodsley's sophisticated London printing house would not have taken too kindly to a Yorkshire parson's busily overseeing its task, as Sterne gives evidence of having done on the occasion of the *Political Romance*: "do not" he wrote to Caesar Ward about the printing of the pamphlet, "at your Peril . . . presume to alter or transpose one Word, nor rectify one false Spelling, nor so much as add or diminish one Comma or Tittle, in or to my *Romance*. . . ."[16] With this in mind, and because I could find no pattern which might have explained it as a printing-house phenomenon, I shall preserve the unique dashing of the York text, in which the usual em, 2-em and 3-em lengths, are supplemented by dashes made up of from two to five hyphens. My assumption is that the printer was attempting to duplicate what he saw in the manuscript, a labor the London printers were unwilling to undertake to indulge Sterne's whimsical desires. The second edition uses standard dash lengths, as do all subsequent editions and all subsequent volumes.[17] Sterne's practice of not using closing quotation marks before the parenthetical introduction of the speaker or of commentary will also be followed, though the second edition "corrects" this punctuation; Sterne's consistency in this practice, particularly in the "Abuses of Conscience"

16. *A Political Romance* (York, 1759), p. 50. Sterne offers a legal excuse for his concern with his text, arguing that "in case any of the Descendents of *Curl* should think fit to invade my Copy-Right, and print it over again in my Teeth, I may not be able, in a Court of Justice, to swear strictly to my own Child, after you had *so large a Share* in the begetting it." Nonetheless, I believe it safe to assume that this humorous legalism is merely a modest cover for Sterne's real interest in the integrity of his text; that he was proud of the *Romance* is attested to by his setting its price at one shilling, since "it is a Web wrought out of my own Brain . . ." (p. 51). Further evidence of Sterne's interest in his text is gathered by Stout, p. 49, n. 3.

17. Hyphens are used for dashes on only two or three occasions in the other volumes; with somewhat more frequency in the sermons; and, interestingly enough, quite often in Lydis Medalle's three volume edition of the *Letters* (London: T. Becket, 1775).

sermon, would necessitate a large scale tampering with the York text.

The second edition of Volumes I and II, adds a Frontispiece by Hogarth, a footnote on p. 134 of Volume I, identifying Heinrich van Deventer as the source of the Memoire on intra-uterine baptism, and a dedication to William Pitt; both the dedication and the plate occur in two states. Obvious typographical errors are corrected, but others are introduced. There are a few substantive alterations, none of which clearly indicates Sterne's hand. For example, in Volume I, "without any opposition" (p. 26) becomes "without opposition"; "But it is certain" (p. 36) becomes "But it is as certain"; and "grave and serious" (p. 56) becomes "grave or serious." The alterations in Volume II are equally indifferent: "and a fertile source of obscurity is it" (p. 15) becomes "and a fertile source of obscurity it is"; and "even a wanting in points in common honesty" (p. 138) becomes "even wanting in points of common honesty." The two alterations in the last phrase are particularly interesting, because they occur within the "Abuses" sermon and restore the readings of the 1750 version. But in no instance can we feel very safe in assigning the correction to Sterne rather than to an alert proofreader or printer; and even the one obvious stylistic improvement, the alteration of the redundancy, "grave and serious," is not beyond a printer's province in the eighteenth century. In short, and the same is true of all nine volumes, there is little evidence that Sterne paid significant attention to the text of *Tristram* after the first edition, though there is enough evidence to tantalize us with the possibility that here and there he did, in Shandean fashion, emend his text.

Volumes I and II were published twice again in 1760; a fifth edition appeared in 1763 and a sixth in 1767. Collation demonstrates only the growing divergence from the first edition as errors accumulate, since the printer's copy in most instances was the prior edition. While the textual value of these editions is negligible, however, some interesting bibliographical problems may be briefly noted. Sheet A of the third edition of Volume I exists in three states; an apprentice apprently set the first version, necessitating press corrections to undo his many errors, one of which (a comma for a period) was not caught until the fifth edition. The third edition of Volume II is most troublesome and presents a problem I have not yet solved. Sheets A-H are identical in all copies examined, and are a complete resetting of the second edition, which was used as the printer's copy. The remaining sheets, I-M$^2$, however, are the same as those used for the second edition, with some alterations and different press figures. This would be simple enough, the evidence indicating that the decision to publish a third edition was made while sheets of the second edition were still in press. The complication arises from the fact that K-M$^2$ exists in three states: state 1 is found in the second edition; state 2 of K is found in some copies of the third edition with state 3 of L-M$^2$; and state 3 of K is found in other copies of the third edition with state 2 of L-M$^2$. I have located only one copy where state 2 of K-M$^2$ is intact,[18] and none where state 3 is intact. State 2 makes a few changes in spelling and punctuation, for example, "lye" for "lay" (p. 161) and "ashes!" for "ashes." (p. 143), which are continued in state 3.[19] State 3 makes an additional effort to replace broken type, to adjust the spacing, and to alter some erratic dash lengths. Most significant are two alterations made in L: "and a half" to "and an half" and "biting his lip" to "biting his lips" (p. 165); and one in M: "had found out" to "has found out" (p. 173). I cannot explain why the second and third states of these sheets were thus mixed, or who

18. I have not been able to examine this copy, held by the Charles Patterson Van Pelt Library of the University of Pennsylvania, but Dr. Neda M. Westlake has checked the variants and press-figures for me, and it would seem that all three sheets are the second state.

19. One error is introduced into state 2 and continues in state 3: "sittting" for "sitting" (p. 143); it occurs in a line where an odd-sized (em+en) dash has been shortened to an em length. The press-figures are different in the three states.

authorized these substantive changes in pages already set.

At any rate, the fourth edition of Volume II was set not from either state of the third, but from the second edition, so that the substantive variants of the third state disappeared from the textual development of *Tristram*. The fourth edition of Volume I was set from the third. The fifth edition of both volumes was set from the fourth and the sixth edition from the fifth. Except for a few very minor stop-press corrections, I have found no variants in the copies of these editions I have collated.

It seems clear to me, then, that the first edition of Volumes I and II, the York edition, is the obvious choice of copy-text for the modern editor; the second edition is of interest primarily in demonstrating the changes Dodsley wrought upon Ann Ward's work, though an editor may be justified in adopting a few substantive variants; the third through sixth editions have importance in that they provide evidence of Sterne's indifference to the subsequent republication of *Tristram* — and insofar as the deterioration of a text is always of some interest to the textual editor.

Volumes III and IV of *Tristram* appeared at the end of January 1761, published by Dodsley. A variant state of the first edition exists with the readings "woulda ciad" for "would a citadel" (p. 160), a closing quotation mark for an incorrect inverted comma (p. 171), and "aud" for "and" (p. 187). The first two readings are from a second state, the third from a first state — which is quite possible since the three variants occur in three different sheets.[20] A second edition of Volume III was published in the same year. The variants seem only marginally significant, though there are many of them, particularly in dash lengths. Of the substantive changes, the most interesting are: "quoth my uncle" corrected to "quoth my father" (p. 19); "catechising at all advantages" corrected to "catching at all advantages" (p. 100); "sad and melancholy" altered to

---

20. I assume the reading "woulda ciad" is the result of dropped type, but it could of course be a compositorial error instead.

"bad and melancholy" (p. 101); "so elegant" altered to "so eloquent" (p. 110), a much better word in context; "grandmother" corrected to "great grandmother" (p. 149); and finally "wet tinder" changed to "*damp* tinder" (p. 188). We have some evidence, I believe, in these changes that Sterne spent a few minutes, albeit a very few, in correcting the first edition. At the same time, it is readily apparent that his interest in doing so is not comparable in any way to the reworkings of Richardson, Smollett or Fielding. Many errors are introduced into the second edition, and several from the first are retained: for example, "these veral receptacles" for "the several receptacles" (p. 88). As with the third edition of Volume II, sheets from the first edition of Volume III are used in the second edition. I-N$^4$ are the same in both, though corrections have been made. In N, the number of lines per page is altered, but even here it appears that the type was not reset, merely shifted.[21]

No declared second edition of Volume IV has ever been found, though a concealed second edition does exist, as Monkman has pointed out:

> This second version ... of volume iv is something of a mystery. It collates identically with the first; and the half-title and title-page may well be the same setting, though the type has shifted slightly. What is certain is that the first ten sheets of the book, B-L$^8$, are complete resettings with different press-figures and with occasional differences of punctuation, capitalization, and some corrections; which is why I call it the second version. Sheets M-P also have different press-figures, but seem to be the same setting with one or two textual errors corrected.[22]

Monkman missed the similar situation in Volume III, but his tentative explanation of Volume IV may well explain both:

> What may have happened [he writes] ... is that during the

21. The press-figures are different except on pages 154 and 177, where not only the figure but its location on the page is the same.
22. Monkman, p. 25.

printing the order was increased; the pages already pulled, of which the type had been distributed, were reset; and a few corrections were made to the pages still in type. Further sheets were then pulled on different presses, which would explain the different press-figures. There may well be better explanations. Perhaps two printing-houses were involved.[23]

Machine collation demonstrates that the first nine rather than ten sheets were reset, L appearing to be the same setting in both editions. It also appears that the Latin version of Slawkenbergius' Tale, which occupies the versos of B-C$^2$, was not reset, though some changes were made. In general, then, we may say that every short cut possible was taken by Dodsley in the printing of this "second edition" (or issue) of Volume IV. As in the earlier volumes, while some typographical errors are corrected, others are introduced, including, as noted by Monkman, the incorrect emendation of *"Baylet"* to *"Bayle"* (p. 118).[24] A substantive variant occurs on p. 137 where "lost his seat" is altered to "lost his hat"; and another on p. 175, where "of its accord" is corrected to "of its own accord." Mysteriously, p. 158 appears to have been reset, but the only alteration is the incorrect "vile of mark Illegitimacy" for the earlier "vile mark of Illegitimacy." The second version of Volume IV appears consistently in sets of *Tristram* with the second edition of Volume III and, as Monkman points out, is quite rare in relation to the first edition.

Volumes V and VI appeared in December 1761 (imprint: 1762); the title-pages indicate that Sterne had changed publishers to T. Becket and P. A. Dehondt. Why he changed is not known, though perhaps it had something to do with Dodsley's handling of the second edition of Volumes III and IV. The second edition of Volumes V and

---

23. *Ibid.* Evidence for this view is supplied by Sterne's letter to Stephen Croft (Feb. 17, 1761): "One half of the town abuse my book as bitterly, as the other half cry it up to the skies — the best is, they abuse and buy it, and at such a rate, that we are going on with a second edition as fast as possible." (*Letters*, pp. 129-30).

24. *Ibid.*; Monkman's citation to p. 188 is an error.

VI was not published until 1767. About Volume VI, little
need be said; only two minor substantive changes are made
and a few more changes in accidentals; the most numerous
changes are in dash lengths. Sterne's hand is nowhere
evident.[25] The second edition of Volume V is another case,
however, since it contains a new motto on the title-page
and two new sentences in the text, the only major
substantive variation from the first edition of *Tristram* in
all subsequent lifetime editions. The new motto is similar
in meaning to those of the first edition, being a response to
those critics who had found the first four volumes
shocking, particularly since the author was a clergyman.[26]
The new sentences are added to the closing section of
chapter 42, the original version of which read:

> The *Danes*, . . . quoth the corporal, who were on the left at the
> siege of *Limerick*, were all auxiliaries.——And very good ones,
> said my uncle *Toby*.—But the auxiliaries, *Trim*, my brother is
> talking about,—I conceive to be different things.—— [P.
> 146.]

Two sentences have been added in the middle of this
discussion:

> . . . And very good ones, said my uncle *Toby*.—And your
> honour roul'd with them, captains with captains.—Very well,
> said the corporal.—But the auxiliaries, my brother is talking

25. Just possibly, the numerous changes in dash lengths are a sign of
Sterne's hand, though this must remain a conjecture. While variants in dash
lengths between editions of the other volumes contain almost an equal number
of those lengthened and those shortened, in Volumes V and VI, about 90 per
cent of the changes of the second edition lengthen the dash by an em. To be
sure, it is impossible to conceive that Sterne indicated the specific dashes he
wanted lengthened, but perhaps he did ask the printer to open up the text in
this way, and the printer lengthened dashes where he could, while preserving
the page by page reprinting. This would suggest, as I believe is the case, that
for Sterne the dash was not important as a grammatical or oratorical sign, but
rather as a visual one — it affects the appearance of the page. At any rate, I
shall preserve the dash lengths of the first edition, at least until a better
explanation of this phenomenon is found — or at least better evidence than a
purely conjectural conversation between author and printer.
26. The new motto reads: "*Si quis Clericus, aut Monachus, verba
joculatoria, visum moventia sciebat anathema esto*" and cites the Second
Council of Carthage. "*visum*" is an obvious misprint for "*risum*."

about, answered my uncle *Toby*,–I conceive to be different things.——

Like the first edition of Volume V, the second edition is signed by Sterne on the first page, the protection he devised in response to imitations, and which he later continued by signing Volumes VII and IX. This signature, the motto, and the two new sentences all lead Monkman to assert that "there is no doubt that Sterne himself had a hand in revising" the first edition; and he specifically affirms that the new sentences "must have been added by Sterne himself."[27] My own inclination would perhaps be more conservative, though ultimately I believe my text will incorporate the changes of the second edition. What disturbs me is the cryptic nature of the new sentences. That Sterne would intrude a private joke or compliment into his text is not to be gainsaid, and surely what we have here has all the markings of a secret gibe at, or perhaps a gracious compliment to, the Danish auxiliaries. But nothing that we know of Sterne suggests why he wanted to make the allusion, and hence its meaning remains somewhat obscure. This obscurity and the uniqueness of such an addition in the textual history of *Tristram* may serve as cautionary brakes to the assurance with which we accept the two new lines as authentic, though at present I certainly have no answer to the obvious question – if Sterne did not add the lines, who did?

The second edition of Volume V offers another problem, for no less than three totally different settings exist, all equally proclaiming themselves to be the second edition. The fact is that only the signed second edition is authentic – and I have found it in sets only with the second edition of Volume VI. The other two settings (which are rarer) always appear in collected sets with a "New Edition," dated 1769, of Volume VI. Collation shows that the true second edition was the printer's copy for one of these spurious second editions, and that it in

27. Monkman, p. 27.

turn was used as printer's copy for the other. Hence we have, in effect, a third and fourth edition of Volume V, both published with a title-page dated 1767, and both declaring themselves second editions.[28] Monkman could find no explanation for this state of affairs, and I too admit defeat. The variants are extensive, but almost solely in the accidentals.

Volumes VII and VIII were published in January 1765, again by Becket and Dehondt; Volume VII is signed by Sterne and contains an errata list on the verso of the title-page. A concealed second edition of VII and VIII, without the signature of Sterne and with the errata corrected, is described by Monkman; it is among the rarest of the lifetime editions of *Tristram* — if indeed it was published during his lifetime. Once more there are numerous variants, but again most are in the accidentals and show no evidence of Sterne's hand. Two of the substantive alterations in Volume VII seem to introduce errors into the text: "I had heard" becomes "I have heard" (p. 17) and "say we" becomes "say she" (p. 57); the original readings are to be preferred. The third alteration corrects the obvious error, "said my uncle *Toby* low to herself" (p. 99). In Volume VIII, "work is it" is altered to "work it is" (p. 3); "make the attack" to "make an attack" (p. 39); "betwixt his" to "between his" (p. 61); "give us as" to "gave us as" (p. 78); and "that pass" to "the pass" (p. 128). These are more substantive variants than we have seen in other volumes, but the changes are indifferent ones, and we can hardly feel secure assigning them to Sterne.

The last volume of *Tristram* was published, again by Becket and Dehondt, in January 1767 and was not reprinted during Sterne's lifetime. As Monkman notes, the

28. The editions may be readily distinguished by the variant readings on p. 87:

| 1st ed. | 2nd ed. | 3rd ed. | 4th ed. |
|---------|---------|---------|---------|
| *Angus*'s | *Augus*'s | *Augus*'s | *Angus*'s |
| *Mackay*'s | *Mackay*'s | *Mackey*'s | *Mackey*'s |

Dedication to Pitt exists in two states, but the variants are of no significance.

These are, then, the volumes of *Tristram Shandy* with which the modern editor must concern himself in preparing his text. A word should be said, however, about the seventh edition of Volume I, which appeared in the year of Sterne's death; it was set from the sixth edition, and contains no evidence of his hand. Since Sterne died in March 1768, and was busy at the time of his death with, if anything, *A Sentimental Journey*, I feel justified in omitting this edition from consideration. Similarly, in preparing my text, I shall not consider the various Dublin piracies during Sterne's lifetime or after;[29] nor the Lynch edition which, in spite of its fradulent title-pages, was published no earlier than 1767, and which offers not the slightest suggestion of Sterne's cooperation; nor will I consider the 1780 collected edition, called by Wilbur Cross "the first attempt at a critical edition,"[30] but which seems to me without any testamentary authority – and, after a close study of its variants, without interest. In brief, the historical collation for the present edition will be limited to the lifetime editions of *Tristram Shandy* which I have already described.

The copy-text for the present edition will be the first edition of all nine volumes; for Volumes I-IV, I have used a Beinecke Library (Yale University) set;[31] for Volumes V-IX, a set in my own collection. Each volume has been collated with at least five other copies, when available, as was the case for the first edition of each volume. Because

---

29. Ian Watt's Riverside edition of *Tristram* (Boston: Houghton Mifflin Co., 1965) lists some "significant variants" from the "Dublin Collected Edition," that is, a seven-volume edition of the *Works* (1779), of which *Tristram* occupies the first three volumes; I have examined several Dublin editions which appeared during Sterne's lifetime and concur with Monkman's statement that they have "no textual value" (p. 30). Watt also lists "significant variants" from the "Lynch" edition, my investigation of which is incomplete (see Cross, p. 600, and Monkman, p. 30).

30. See Cross, pp. 609-611.

31. Pressmark: IM/St 45/759Es.

subsequent editions were line by line reprintings, I was able to use the Hinman collator for the comparison of subsequent editions to the first edition, as well as to each other. Here again, I tried to locate at least five copies for collation, though this was not always possible. Needless to say, more collation could have been done. So closely, however, do my findings concur with Monkman's, and so little does the evidence indicate Sterne's active participation in proofreading, that I believe my plan is sufficient for the particular author and the particular work. That a variant edition may yet turn up is an editor's constant hedge against pride; and when one does turn up, no matter how much an editor has done, his efforts may be rendered insufficient.

In addition to the many volumes I was able to examine in Monkman's extensive collection at Shandy Hall, I have collated copies from seventeen other libraries in the United States and England. The University of Florida now has five sets of *Tristram* containing lifetime editions; one is a complete set of first editions owned by Thackeray, Leslie Stephen and Virginia Woolf; it is unmarked. Finally, I have two sets in my own possession. The rarest of the lifetime volumes would seem to be the unique copy of Volume II, third edition, described earlier; the second state of Volume I, third edition (the University of Minnesota library has the only copy I have been able to locate);[32] the variant state of the first edition of Volume III (I have the only copy I have seen; Monkman has located another since I last worked with his collection); the third state of Volume V, second edition (Yale has two copies; Monkman one); and the concealed second edition of Volumes VII and VIII.[33] The

---

32. The states may be readily distinguished by the variant readings on p. 15:

| state 1 | state 2 | state 3 |
|---|---|---|
| disasterosu | disasterosu | disasterous |
| clipplings | clippings | clippings |

33. In one of the vagaries which makes book-collecting interesting, in 1970 I was able to purchase a set containing the concealed second edition of Volumes VII and VIII for the University of Florida Library and another for

York edition of Volumes I and II must also be considered somewhat rare; and I have wanted to purchase for several years without success the third and fourth editions of I and II, though I had no difficulty in locating sufficient copies of both for collation.

The printer's copy for the edition will be photocopies of the actual pages of the copy-text. An editor's experience is largely one of trial and error, and one of the most time-consuming errors I made was the attempt to emend a modern printed text (the Ian Watt edition) for my printer's copy, despite warnings from predecessors that this should not be done. I must now express my total agreement with them; the compounding of errors is the only outcome to be expected from this method of preparing printer's copy, no matter how careful one tries to be. The primary printer's problem with using the actual pages of *Tristram* is the long "s," but I have been assured that our printer can deal with it. Dash lengths of the original will be copied as closely as possible, as will the various devices and typographical oddities that Sterne so delighted in. Most important, we will try to spread the text out, in an effort to reproduce more closely the original experience of *Tristram*. It is worth remembering that the original page contained about 750 characters on twenty lines, while most modern reprints will have some 2,400 characters on forty lines. Obviously, the two pages look quite different, for the openness and freedom of Sterne's page is lost. We will use a thirty-line page, with approximately 1,500 characters, leaded three points; we hope this will restore something of the appearance of the original, without becoming prohibitively expensive. The text will be published in two volumes, with the textual apparatus gathered at the end of the second. A third volume will contain the annotations. While this last arrangement is not wholly satisfactory, it makes possible two things we most

---

my own collection, while Monkman searched for many years before finding his copy. Yale has two copies, while UCLA has a second edition of Volume VIII in a set with the first edition of Volume VII.

desire: a clean page of text and a convenient location of annotative materials. Because of the kind of work *Tristram* is, we were faced with a few lines of text at times demanding several pages of annotation. While a separate volume of annotation is not as convenient as *foot*notes, it is certainly better than *back*notes; the scholar, for whom the edition is primarily designed, should have little trouble in keeping the third volume by his side as he reads the text — and the text will be uncluttered by commentary he may feel is irrelevant to his interests or damaging to his pleasure.

The textual apparatus will consist of four major sections. The first will contain the discursive textual notes, primarily for the explanation of editorial decisions for which the rationale may not be evident. The second section will list all emendations to the copy text and will be divided for substantives and accidentals. The appearance of these changes in subsequent lifetime editions will also be recorded. The third section will contain the record of editorial decisions on line-end hyphenation. The final section will list the textual variants in the lifetime editions; all substantive and accidental variants from the second edition, not noted in the list of emendations, will be listed here; and the substantive variants of the other lifetime editions will also be recorded. Appendices will be used as required for dealing with several special problems such as the Deventer "Memoire."[34]

This then is the basic plan I propose to follow in editing *Tristram Shandy*. In the remaining few minutes, I would like to return to my starting point, the problematic nature of editing, for although I have not finished the actual preparation of the text, I can readily provide from the first volume, alone, sufficient illustrations of the way in which

34. This arrangement owes much to G. Thomas Tanselle's essay "Some Principles for Editorial Apparatus," *Studies in Bibliography*, 25 (1972), 41-88. My primary deviation is in my giving the historical collation within the list of emendations and not repeating the information in the historical collation list; I do not find this practice as inconvenient or confusing as Tanselle does.

practice baffles plan; illustrations of the fact that, like
Uncle Toby with his maps, I have been often perplexed:
"'Twas not by ideas,—by heaven! his life was put in
jeopardy by words."

For example, does one emend "But it is certain at the
same time," following a sentence which begins "I know
very well," to "But it is as certain at the same time . . ."
(p. 36)? To be sure, if Sterne had shown evidence of
polishing the first edition with any thoroughness, we might
easily agree to do so. But the second edition of Volume I,
where the change first occurs (and it continues in all
subsequent editions) shows, as suggested above, only
minimal evidence of Sterne's hand. It is a better reading,
perhaps, but only a shade better at most. Similarly, should
one emend "he had so shrewd guess at the weaknesses
etc." to the obviously more idiomatic "so shrewd a guess"
(p. 119)? One might feel more comfortable here in making
the change, though the fact is that the first four editions
all printed "so shrewd guess"; the change occurs in the
fifth edition. Or again, the phrase, "both the one and
other" which is altered from the second edition onward to
"both the one and the other" (p. 133) — should this
phrase be emended? Each instance is different to be sure,
though each involves one omitted word. My own inclination has been to emend the first; to follow the copy-text
for the second; and to emend the last, though indicating in
a textual note the occurence of the phrasing "a stroke of
one or other of 'em" in Volume V (p. 75).

One of the most complex problems of the first volume
of *Tristram* involves the "Memoire" of the Sorbonne
doctors, one of several instances where Sterne interpolates
extensive quoted material into his text. While the reasons
for my conclusions are too involved to describe here (and I
have written about them elsewhere),[35] suffice it to say that
I decided that the copy-text for the "Memoire" should not
be the text of the first edition, but rather the text of the

35. Forthcoming in *Publications of the Bibliographical Society of
America*.

"Memoire" as it appeared in the 1734 edition of Deventer's *Observations*, which Sterne cites as his source in the second edition, and which, I believe, he actually tried to copy verbatim. Indeed, much of the wit of the "Memoire's" inclusion in *Tristram* lies in the fact that Sterne could use it verbatim, that it was not a fiction but the historical record of an actual deliberation. This being the case, we can even guess that, had Sterne had photo-reproductive processes available to him, he would have used them to provide a printer's copy. Moreover, by using Deventer as copy-text, the modern editor can then highlight the few substantive alterations that Sterne did make; to do so leads to the conclusion, for example, that the reading of the first edition *"sans faire aucun tort a le pere"* (p. 140), is the one Sterne wanted, rather than the more "correct" reading of the second edition *"au pere"* or the unfortunate correction of the third and subsequent editions, *"à la mere."*[36] In this instance, I believe a carefully prepared text will, by preserving Sterne's "inaccurate" French, preserve not only a fine Shandean joke, but as well the careful manner in which he prepared for it.

The emendation of accidentals can also cause problems as we all know, and often the time spent on a spelling or a punctuation mark is in inverse proportion to its significance. Let me illustrate in the case of spelling. Should we preserve the first edition's "nicity" (p. 41), which is to be sure a possible spelling variation, or should we alter it to the more common "nicety," the spelling Sterne uses 109 pages later? Should we preserve the spelling "enew," since

---

36. The major substantive change of Deventer's "sans préjudicier à la mere" (*Observations Importantes sur le Manuel des Accouchemens* ... *Traduite du Latin de M. Henry de Deventer* [Paris, 1734], p. 367) to *"sans faire aucun tort a la mere"* (p. 137), echoing precisely an earlier occurrence of the phrase, prepares for Sterne's joke: "provided ... That the thing can be done ... *sans faire aucun tort a le pere"* (p. 140). In all copies of the first edition I have examined, the leaf on which this occurs is a cancel, and I agree with a suggestion made to me by Monkman that quite possibly the York compositor also corrected what seemed to him a blatant error, and Sterne insisted on a reprinting to preserve his carefully structured joke.

it is a possible Northern dialect variation of "enow" (p. 65), or is "enew" merely a typographical error? Should we change the possessive "ordinaries" to "ordinary's" as it occurs twenty-five pages later; and does what we do in this instance have any bearing on "farmers sons" (p. 105) where the possessive apostrophe is again missing? Should we preserve "errors" of the first edition like "thy ears" for "thine ears" and "thou will" for "thou wilt" (p. 64), the former of which is corrected only after the fourth edition, the latter in the second edition? It is one thing to say that the accidentals will be taken from the first edition and another to perpetuate a printer's errors, or the printer's inability to distinguish between "l" and "t" in Sterne's manuscript. Examples of this sort can be multiplied to considerable length, but I hope my point has been sufficiently established. The evidence we can bring to bear on such problems is as varied as the problems themselves and often produces contradictory results. We can consider Sterne's handwriting, as evidenced in letters, in the holograph of the Rabelaisian fragment, written, I believe, about the same time as Volumes I and II, or in the surviving manuscripts of *A Sentimental Journey*. We can consider the alterations made in subsequent editions; the fact that "enew" was not altered until the fifth edition, while "nicity" was changed in the second, may be useful information for the editor. And we can also consult the evidence of Sterne's usage in other instances, as in the case of "nicity" and "ordinary's," though here we must also consider whether our particular author is consistent or inconsistent in spelling and pointing — and Sterne demonstrates no penchant for consistency. Finally, the historical evidence of usage in Sterne's time, particularly in the north of England, and the printing practices of Ann Ward, Dodsley, and Becket and Dehondt, may also prove useful. In short, as does any other editor, I will sift through a welter of evidence, carefully weigh one alternative against the other, and then make my guess as to what Sterne wanted; and I will record the rejected alternatives so that

future scholars will have the material available to engage in
that most delightful of intellectual pursuits — second
guessing.

When I first began to sound out Sterneans about the
possibility of a Sterne edition, I had two experiences
which perhaps say as much about editing as any volume on
the subject. Because I was most interested in annotating
*Tristram*, I searched long and hard for a textual editor.
Finally I found someone who expressed some interest; but
after his initial favorable response, when I explained in
more detail what I thought the textual problems would be,
I never heard from him again — or almost never, for about
a year ago his publisher sent me, I assume at his request,
his study of Samuel Beckett. Three years ago, when I
actually set to work on the project, Professor Louis Landa
asked me how long I thought it would take to complete.
"Five years" I responded, at which Landa shook his
knowledgeable head and replied, "young man, you are an
optimist" — which was, to be sure, a generous evaluation
of my ignorance. Now, as the days and hours fly over my
head "like light clouds of a windy day, never to return
more" — as Tristram remarks in one of his most serious
moments — I can well understand the urgency of his
response to the press of time and Jenny's graying locks:
"Heaven have mercy upon us both" — and may I add,
upon editors as well.

# "Of making many books there is no end": Editing Smollett

## O M Brack, Jr.

If asked what I would prescribe for a paroxysm likely to terminate in some form of editorial activity, I would always recommend Vinton A. Dearing's "Methods of Textual Editing"[1] — read twice, with a large libation, and if the symptoms persist, see me in the morning. His is a witty, urbane essay filled with commonsense advice and warnings for the would-be editor; one reads the essay with an increased sense of the difficulties of textual editing but with the growing confidence (particularly if one is young) that if one follows the eight processes as outlined one will attain "wisdom, knowledge, and joy," the latter presumably on the publication of the text. But, alas, "vanity of vanities, saith the Preacher, vanity of vanities; all is vanity." Now I do not wish to argue that the Preacher was in fact a textual editor, although a case might be made for it, nor do I wish to impugn Professor Dearing's fine essay, since he does warn the neophyte that "textual editing is a

---

1. Originally delivered at a seminar on bibliography held at the William Andrews Clark Library, University of California at Los Angeles, 12 May 1962. Reprinted in *Bibliography and Textual Criticism*, ed. O M Brack, Jr. and Warner Barnes (Chicago, 1969), pp. 73-101.

long, exacting, and often monotonous task" and implies
that the joy, if there is to be any, may well be in heaven.
"So little do we accustom ourselves to consider the effects
of time, that things necessary and certain often surprise us
like unexpected contingencies."[2] The often overlooked
fact is that even if one explores the implications of the
editorial project as thoroughly as possible before it is
begun, as Dearing suggests, and sets limits to the work so
that it may in time be ended, though not completed, as
Samuel Johnson suggests, numerous problems will arise
which will make it necessary to extend the "reasonable
time" originally allotted. From my own experience, and my
observations of other large editorial projects, this statement seems axiomatic, and it might be useful, perhaps, to
add a ninth process: after calculating the reasonable time
necessary to complete the given editorial project, multiply
the amount of time by a factor of two — at least. This will
prevent a great "vexation of spirit," particularly when one
is asked (for what seems to be the ten-thousandth time)
the publication date of such and such a volume. Ye who
listen with credulity to the whispers of fancy, and pursue
with eagerness the phantoms of hope; who expect that age
will perform the promises of youth, and that the deficien-
cies of the present day will be supplied by the morrow;
attend the history of the Smollett edition.

I would like to be able to state that the Smollett edition
had its auspicious beginning when I had as it were a strange
kind of feeling stealing over me . . . so strong, I imagined
that a pen was in my right hand, and a voice crying "Edit!
Edit!"[3] or when I beheld a many-faced flying whatnot
descending from the heavens in a cloud of fire and dancing
on the firmament,[4] but the beginning was much more
prosaic — in keeping with Smollett. The commitment of
what now appears to be fifteen years of my life (I hope
that I do not have to double *this* figure!) to a major

2. *Idler*, No. 43.
3. William McGonagall, *Poetic Gems*.
4. Jeremy Feeble, *The Travelling Companion; or, Did he but Dare*.

editorial undertaking happened so casually that when I
came to write this section of my paper I had to spend
several hours in the office reading proposals and correspondence, not only to try to reconstruct the series of
events, but to find out what year the project began! (I
made the distressing discovery that it started one year
earlier than I had remembered.) During the fall of 1965,
my first year at the University of Iowa, I became
acquainted with Robert Scholes and over coffees and
lunches we discussed one of our mutual interests, prose
narratives, and at some point our conversation turned to
*Roderick Random* on the impetus, as I recall, of the
publication of a new edition of the work the year before
with an afterword by John Barth. For some reason (I wish
that I remembered why — probably some sort of bibliographical fever contracted during my stay in Austin and
Bob's in Charlottesville), we decided that what the
scholarly world was really waiting for (and still is) was
(you guessed it) a critical edition of the Works of Tobias
George Smollett. We discussed the idea with the late Curt
Zimansky; he asked some hard questions (to which, I
suppose, we thought we had the answers) and was opposed
to the project only mildly — Curt's own special way of
signifying approval. Curt supplied me with the name and
address of the dean of Smollettians, Lewis M. Knapp, and I
wrote to him 13 February 1966 to get his reaction to the
project and to ask if he would be interested in becoming
involved in the edition, assuming, of course, that there was
one, and if he knew of any others who shared our
enthusiasm for Smollett. He wrote back, declining an
active role because of other scholarly commitments and
age, pointed out that the other scholars who had written
on Smollett had either shifted their interests or were at an
age when they too would be reluctant to make such a long
range commitment, and offered me one name, Thomas R.
Preston. We communicated by letter and telephone and
agreed on the obvious: it was pointless to think about
doing an edition without a substantial amount of money,

and neither of us was sure how or where any could be obtained. Much of the spring of 1966 was spent conferring with people in the University of Iowa's Department of Publications and writing letters to anyone I could think of who might assist me in attempting to ascertain the likely cost of the edition. I then spent a month in the summer visiting libraries trying to determine how many editions of each work would have to be collated and how many of the editions had been revised. On my return I used this information to draw up a tentative budget to submit to the Graduate College of the University of Iowa in hopes of securing funds. The good angels, or evil angels, depending on your point of view or, perhaps, I should say, my mood, went to work and persuaded the Graduate Dean that the edition should be funded. On 17 November 1966 I received a letter formally committing the University to support of the project, and the fun began.

At the outset there were major problems to be resolved, and I realize now I should have heeded the characters obscure above the gate and not entered without solutions well in hand. I think that I knew this at the time, although I may be flattering myself, but I found it difficult to commit several years of my life to preparations for a project whose future seemed very much in doubt. Had the edition not materialized I would have regretted spending the time I did, but since it did materialize, I wish that I had spent more time in preparation, and so we have come full circle, feeling a bit like Olivier's Hamlet. One of the major problems was the canon. I had neatly sidestepped the issue in my original proposal by including only the five novels, the *Travels through France and Italy* and suggesting that the *History and Adventures of an Atom* and a miscellaneous volume or two might be included. The open-ended edition, of course, was a sign of the times — the days when the ambrosial fragrance of money filled all academe with a sense of new joy ineffable. It was clear from the first that this was not to be the *complete* works, and I categorically eliminated all of Smollett's translations, compilations and historical works, as well as the poems and plays, feeling strongly at the time that it was by virtue of the seven works mentioned in the proposal, particularly the best novels, that he was still read and enjoyed. Although it sounds as if the limitations placed on the edition were made on aesthetic grounds, and they were in part, they served at least two other functions: they eliminated the areas in which attributions to Smollett are extremely difficult, and they kept the finances of the edition within calculable figures, or so I hoped. I also realized that if one was going to make any pretense of producing an edition of Smollett's works, there had to be a minimum number of works included that were consistent with its proposed audience's expectations, and there had to be enough money to see the volumes through to completion. The miscellaneous volume or two was obviously a hedge against having overlooked some work for which a good argument could be made for inclusion, but initially I must confess that my mind became tyrannized by airy notions which forced it to hope beyond the limits of sober probability. Tantalized by Derek Roper's discovery of a marked copy of the first volume of the *Critical Review* identifying the early contributors and by a footnote in Lewis M. Knapp's biography suggesting that at least two and, perhaps four, sets of the *Critical* had the contributors identified,[5] I rioted in the fancy of producing a volume of Smollett's criticism. It is with pain I recall how I was tempted from my path into the slough of attribution and the hours spent trying to locate one of these sets, without which the task of identifying Smollett's contributions proved impossible. Perhaps some future editor will discover one of the marked sets or will refine a technique for distinguishing Smollett's journalistic style from the many similar ones in the period, but until then a

---

5. Derek Roper, "Smollett's 'Four Gentlemen': The First Contributors to the *Critical Review*," *Review of English Studies*, 10 (1959), 38-44; Lewis M. Knapp, *Tobias Smollett: Doctor of Men and Manners* (Princeton, 1949), p. 173 n. 7.

substantial and, no doubt, interesting portion of his
literary output remains unidentified. Despite the initial
failure on this front, two volumes have been added.
Professor Byron Gassman argued persuasively for the
inclusion of *The Briton* in the edition, and it was decided
that this volume would be filled out with the poems and
plays, and earlier misgivings about the inclusion of
translations were overcome as it became increasingly
apparent that Smollett's translation of René Lesage's
*Adventures of Gil Blas*, a work which has become a literary
classic in its own right and is of major importance in
understanding Smollett, could not reasonably be excluded.

Before looking into the difficulties of Smollett's texts,
two other problems might be glanced at briefly. The first is
the assembling and collation of the texts. In the preliminary stages of the edition, after receiving some money,
I wrote to the major libraries requesting a xerox copy of
their Smollett holdings before 1800 in the card catalogue.
When all of the cards were assembled and filed, I
discovered that none of the libraries could be said to have
an important Smollett collection, which meant that there
was no one place I could go to do the bulk of the
bibliographical work. Almost every one had a first edition
of *Humphry Clinker*, and many had first editions of the
other works, particularly the novels, but later editions
were almost non-existent. Even the best collections, that at
Yale and the one assembled by Lewis M. Knapp, had gaps
in their holdings of later editions. Over several years I have
located at least one copy of most of these editions, but
several have been quite elusive. One such was the fourth
edition of *Roderick Random*, printed in 1000 copies by
William Strahan[6] and published in November 1754 with a
1755 date on the title page. This is a crucial edition,
because the famous *Apologue* appears for the first time,
and, as I rightly suspected, it is the last edition revised by
the author. All other investigations having been in vain, I

6. British Museum Add. MSS 48802A, opening 9.

made one last desperate effort to locate a copy by placing a query in the *Book Collector*. In a short time I received a letter from Mr. John Emerson of Lowestoft, Suffolk, describing a copy in his possession. I quickly replied excitedly explaining the importance of the edition, my willingness to pay his personal expenses to the nearest place the book could be microfilmed and offering, of course, to pay for the microfilm. He replied that the obvious solution to the problem was to post the book to me, which he had done. The volumes arrived several weeks later, but during that period I had many dreams of conflagrations, earthquakes, sinking ships and crashing airplanes. Only one state of one edition, so far as I know, has eluded my search. In the first edition of *Roderick Random* each of the two volumes has one cancelled leaf, and I have not seen a copy of volume two in the original state. Fortunately, Luella F. Norwood in preparing her bibliographical dissertation on Smollett had seen a copy and recorded the reading.[7] Thus, after seven years, one of the preliminary processes has not been completed, since I am still searching for a text.

Although it was generally known that Smollett did on occasion revise his works, it was not entirely clear how many of the works to be included in the edition had been revised and to what extent. After my preliminary survey, I was confident that I knew which editions had been revised, but in the short time I had at the various libraries working alone it was impossible to predict accurately the extent of the revisions. The revisions will be discussed in more detail when I take up the individual texts, but, in summary, it might be pointed out that in the two known instances of revision, the *Travels through France and Italy* and the

7. Unpublished dissertation (Yale University, 1931), "A Descriptive Bibliography with Notes Bibliographical and Biographical of the Creative Works of Tobias Smollett, M.D., 1746-1771, with the Posthumous Ode to Independence," pp. 59-60. Norwood, *CBEL*, and *NCBEL* list a number of editions that I am convinced never existed. These problems will be taken up in the textual introductions to the various volumes.

*Adventures of Peregrine Pickle*, used to predict the amount
of time (and, hence, the money) necessary for collation, I
was misled as to the extent of the revisions. In the case of
the *Travels*, Smollett's revisions were not nearly as heavy
as they were in his earlier works, *Roderick Random* and
*Peregrine Pickle*, and in the case of the latter, Howard S.
Buck's apparently detailed collation of the first and second
editions in the appendix to his *A Study in Smollett,
Chiefly "Peregrine Pickle"*[8] proved to be about fifty per
cent inaccurate. Ten editions of *Roderick Random* and
five editions of *Peregrine Pickle* were collated twice, and,
because of the large number of variants, tabulation went
slowly. Even after two collations, I thought that the
incidence of error was too high, and I had all of the
substantive texts, the first four editions of *Roderick
Random*, and the first two editions of *Peregrine Pickle*,
collated again. This was not only very time consuming, but
it destroyed my budget. The next biennium found me
back asking for additional funds to complete the collations
of the other works.

The other problem discretion will allow me only to
touch upon, although it has probably caused greater delays
to the edition than any other factor. The difficulties in
assembling personnel for the Smollett edition were pecu-
liar from the start. There was not in 1965, nor is there
now, any clearly defined body of Smollett scholars, as
there are Johnson or Shakespeare scholars, for example,
and, as I mentioned earlier, Professor Knapp supplied me
with only one name. Since names did not immediately leap
to mind, how was I to assemble an editorial staff? My
procedure was not much different from the way English
departments have recruited faculty in the past. I wrote to
senior colleagues in the field and to friends to ask for
recommendations. After I had a small list of people, I
looked at their previous publications, their professed
interests, and on the basis of this information and an

8. (New Haven, 1925), pp. 123-207.

interview I tried to ascertain if they would be likely to do the editorial work I expected.[9] I felt that I had to go with younger scholars, because there seemed to be little interest in the edition among the more established scholars. The difficulties with having a staff of younger scholars are that one must choose them on the basis of promise, which may not be fulfilled, and that their progress on their volume is likely to be slow, because they have heavier teaching loads and do not receive the large grants and leaves of absence awarded to more senior scholars. It is sad to note that of the seven people assigned volumes in my November 1967 essay in *Books at Iowa* announcing the edition, only two are left, and several have come and gone since. Happily Smollett stock has risen sharply in recent years, and I now have a relative abundance of high-quality volunteers eager to edit volumes.

The textual problems in Smollett's works vary widely in their complexity. The texts of *Ferdinand Count Fathom* and *Sir Launcelot Greaves*, for example, present relatively few problems. The sight collations of all editions through the first posthumous one for each of these works turned up few variants and none which could not be considered as compositorial and hence unauthoritative. That Smollett chose not to revise these works is not too surprising, since neither was well received by the reviewers or the reading public, and his financial condition was never good enough to allow him to spend much time on unprofitable enterprises. It is also possible that he felt them "unworthy the pen of Dr. Smollett."[10] While these texts did not

9. The volume editors are providing the general introductions and historical annotations; the texts are being edited by me with the assistance of a former student or two. The procedures that each editor should follow in preparing his volume have been outlined in Brack, *Rules and Procedures for Editing the Bicentennial Edition of the Works of Tobias Smollett* (Iowa City, 1968). A few modifications have been made in these procedures in the course of preparing the early volumes for the press.

10. *Sir Launcelot Greaves* first appeared serially in the *British Magazine* from January 1760 to December 1761 and was published as a book about 1 April 1762. The work received little critical attention, and the *Monthly Review* [26 (May 1762), 241], for example, devoted only one sentence to it in

provide me with any difficult bibliographical or textual problems, my work on *Ferdinand Count Fathom* did produce an important discovery previously unknown, at least to me. The first edition was published about 15 February 1753 by "W. Johnston, at the Golden Ball in St. Paul's Church-yard,"[11] and, although there is a substantial amount of information on the publication of Smollett's works in William Strahan's printing ledgers, there is no record of his having printed this edition. There is some likelihood that he did, I might add, since he was certainly a silent partner in its publication, having purchased from Smollett a 1/3 share for £40 on 8 November 1752.[12] But I found another entry in Strahan's ledgers of even more interest. In the same year there was a Dublin edition published by Robert Main, who had also published the first Dublin edition of *Peregrine Pickle* in 1751. Under Johnston's account dated 27 April 1753 is the following entry: "For 1/3 of Fathom money from Main £5-5-0."[13] Although this entry is rather cryptic, it would appear that Main had agreed either to pay the London publishers for the privilege of printing the novel in Dublin or to share the profits made from the edition with them.[14] It seems certain in this case, probable in the case of *Peregrine Pickle* and possible in the case of the other works, that the Dublin edition is authoritative and not a piracy. Fortunately I surmised the meaning of this entry in time to include the Dublin editions in the collations. Collecting these editions and tabulating the variants after the collations were made consumed more time, not to mention the additional costs of photocopies and personnel. I would like to be able to announce after all this additional effort

the monthly catalogue: "Better than the common Novels, but unworthy the pen of Dr. Smollett." See Knapp, p. 244.

11. Knapp, pp. 151-153.

12. British Museum Add. MSS 48205, under "Ferdinand."

13. British Museum Add. MSS 48800, opening 135.

14. See the unpublished dissertation (University of Michigan, 1960) by Robert D. Harlan, "William Strahan: Eighteenth Century London Printer and Publisher," p. 68.

that we made an earth-shattering discovery proving that no one making any pretense of producing a critical edition can now afford to ignore Dublin editions, but this also was vanity and vexation of spirit. We discovered no evidence that Smollett took advantage of these editions to make corrections or revisions.

Smollett's two plays, *The Regicide* (1749) and *The Reprisal* (1757), present few textual difficulties, since in each case there seems to have been only one London edition during the author's lifetime, and both editions appear to have been accurately printed.[15] His early satires, *Advice* (1746) and *Reproof* (1747), are also relatively uncomplicated since each of the poems appeared in only one edition before being collected together in slightly revised form in 1748. They were not reprinted again until *Plays and Poems* in 1777. A number of the poems, however, offer a variety of problems. "The Tears of Scotland," for example, seems to have first appeared *c.* 1746 in a small four-page pamphlet, but this text does not represent the final version of the poem. Howard S. Buck pointed out in his *Smollett as Poet* that what has come to be considered as the standard version seems to have first appeared in a collection edited by Thomas Warton called *The Union: or Select Scots and English Poems*, Edinburgh, 1753.[16] Did Smollett make these revisions? It is possible that Smollett learned that Warton was to include his poem in the collection and conveyed his revisions to him. It is also possible that Smollett revised the poem sometime between 1746 and 1753 and reprinted it in some form hitherto undiscovered, and that this was Warton's source for the poem. The poem remained anonymous in *The Union* until the third edition of 1766, possibly, Buck

15. The *Cambridge Bibliography of English Literature* (1940), II, p. 524 and the *New Cambridge Bibliography* (1969), II, column 963, list a 1758 edition of *The Reprisal*, but an extensive search has failed to locate a copy. The 1776 edition is designated on the title-page as the second edition. There was a Dublin edition in 1761 and a Belfast edition in 1767.

16. (New Haven, 1927), pp. 24-25. This 'Edinburgh' edition was probably published in Oxford.

suggests, because of the political sentiments expressed in it. But the reason for its anonymity may simply be that Warton was not certain of its authorship. If the latter conjecture is correct, there would be no reason to believe that Smollett made the revisions specifically for *The Union*. "The Tears of Scotland" was one of the more popular poems of the period and would have been an obvious choice for a collection such as this. Should an earlier publication of the poem in the standard version be discovered which could definitely be connected with Smollett, the problem would be solved, but this is unlikely to happen. The fact that these revisions are the kind of small changes Smollett was fond of making in other works, and one's feeling that they improve the poem must be weighed against the known proclivity of editors of the period to print things to suit themselves.

There is also a strong possibility that "The Tears of Scotland" was revised for one of its musical settings, as both Lewis M. Knapp and Otto Erich Deutsch have shown,[17] and Warton may have gotten his version of the poem from one of these sources. Working with poetry preserved in music presents a whole series of new problems. In the first place, song collections from the eighteenth century are quite rare, and many have disappeared. Secondly, even when a poem is discovered in a collection, the song is often impossible to date. For these reasons, the authority of specific variant forms of a poem set to music must be highly conjectural. Further, some of the more popular poems must have had some history of oral transmission, and it is likely that many of the poems were revised slightly to fit the music and make them more suitable for vocal rendition. Since it is known that the poem in Chapter XL of *Roderick Random* which begins "When Sappho struck the quiv'ring wire" is a shortened

17. Lewis M. Knapp, "Smollett's Verses and their Musical Settings in the Eighteenth Century," *Modern Language Notes*, 46 (1931), 224-32; Otto Erich Deutsch, "Poetry Preserved in Music: Bibliographical Notes on Smollett and Oswald, Handel, and Hayden," *Modern Language Notes*, 63 (1948), 73-88.

and revised version of a poem set to music by James
Oswald and first published in the *Universal Harmony* of
1745, Smollett's authority for the revisions in the poems
set to music cannot be discounted.

The most difficult problem facing the editor of the
poems is the decisions concerning the canon. Only the
separately published poems and the poems appearing in
the novels can be attributed to Smollett with any degree of
certainty. The four lyrics from the *British Magazine* —
"Ode to Blue-Ey'd Ann," "Ode to Sleep," "Ode to Mirth,"
and "To fix her — 'twere a task as vain" — have all been
attributed to Smollett solely on the authority of the
anonymous editor of *Plays and Poems*, 1777. One may
agree with Buck that "for a writer of Smollett's position
and facility . . . a group of but four fugitive pieces is a
preposterously scanty allowance,"[18] but it would be
extremely difficult to attribute verses in the *British
Magazine* to Smollett on the basis of internal evidence.
Smollett's verse is in many ways so typical of the
occasional verse of the period that it is virtually impossible
to recognize. After reading through the verses in the
*British Magazine*, it is difficult to understand why Buck
attempted to attribute to Smollett the three poems he did,
since there seem to be many more candidates for Smollett's authorship which could be accepted into the canon
on the basis of similar arguments. Buck's procedure is
hazardous indeed, and it seems unlikely that any new
attributions can be made without some good external
evidence.

Several of the texts can be passed over quickly. There
was only one edition of the *History and Adventures of an
Atom*, and the confusion surrounding the various issues of
this edition has now been resolved.[19] The *Briton* does not
appear to have been very popular and does not have the
complex transmission of the frequently reprinted perio-

18. *Smollett as Poet*, p. 57.
19. See Brack, "*The History and Adventures of an Atom*, 1769," *Papers
of the Bibliographical Society of America*, 64 (1970), 336-38.

dicals such as the *Spectator* and the *Tatler*. Only seven sets appear to have survived, and none of these contain all thirty-eight numbers; a preliminary examination shows that only the second number was reset.

In the case of *Humphry Clinker*, a succession of bibliographers has attempted to sort out the early editions and variant states. Professor William B. Todd, after examining some thirty copies of the various "editions" of 1771 and 1772, established the precedence of the true editions but concluded that the question in some of its particulars remained unresolved.[20] As fascinating as this puzzle is for analytical bibliographers, the textual editor, I am convinced, need concern himself only with the first edition. The first edition of the novel contains few errors, even in the Win Jenkins passages, which suggests to me that someone went over the novel very carefully. Since it was Smollett's usual habit to read proof, at least on the first printings of his works, one would assume that he had done so in this instance. The difficulty is that Smollett left England in the fall of 1768 and arrived in Italy late that year or early the next; so little is known about these last years of his life that one can only hazard a calculated guess as to whether he saw proofs or had an opportunity to revise his last novel. There appears to have been time to send the proofs to Italy. Professor Knapp argues that the novel was completed in early 1770 and, if this was the case, there was approximately a year before the work was published on 15 June 1771. The book was first announced, however, in the *London Chronicle* for 19-22 January and also 22-24 January 1771: "In the Press, and speedily will be published, In Two Volumes. The Expedition of Humphrey [sic] Clinker. . . ." One of the things that this curious announcement might indicate is that by

20. "Bibliography and the Editorial Problem in the Eighteenth Century," *Studies in Bibliography*, 4 (1951), 50-51, reprinted in Brack and Barnes, pp. 148-49. A more detailed discussion appears in Todd's unpublished dissertation (University of Chicago, 1949), "The Number and Order of Certain Eighteenth-Century Editions," pp. 48-50, 131-35.

January part of the book had been printed, and its final
publication was delayed until June because of Smollett's
insistence that he see the proofs. But what about the plan
to issue the work in two volumes rather than three, as was
subsequently done? Did Smollett send additional materials
to be included in the novel, thus throwing off the initial
calculation? Without some new piece of external evidence
this will never be known. Another explanation, and the
one I find most acceptable at the moment, is that the
partners in the publication, William Johnston and Benjamin Collins, decided to divide the 33 duodecimo sheets
into three slender volumes rather than two fat ones,
thereby increasing their profits.[21] While there is some
evidence that Smollett read proof on *Humphry Clinker*,
there is little reason to believe that he ever revised it. As I
mentioned earlier, the first edition was published 15 June
1771, and the author's ten complimentary copies probably
did not reach him in Italy until July or August. The
reprinting of the work began in July and was completed in
August. Smollett died 17 September. There is no evidence
that he saw copies or any notices of the work before he
died, and there is no reason to think that any of the
variant readings found in the second edition are anything
but compositorial corruptions, except two.[22] Close to the
end of the novel, the date of Matthew Bramble's letter to
Dr. Lewis dated 26 October has been changed to 25
October, and Jery Milford's letter to Sir Watkin Phillips
dated 8 November has been changed to 14 November.
Franklin B. Newman has argued, for example, that this
change was made by Smollett, or by a discerning reader, in
order to rectify a chronological inaccuracy and to allow
the proper time to elapse between the publication of the

21. From the publication of *Roderick Random* (1748), one volume of a
Smollett novel in this format sold for 3 shillings bound, hence an increase in
the price of the novel from 6 shillings to 9 shillings. See Norwood. The entry
for *Humphry Clinker* taken from Benjamin Collins' account book is reprinted
in full in Charles Welsh, *A Bookseller of the Last Century* (London, 1885), pp.
357-58.
22. See Knapp, pp. 279-96.

banns and the marriages.[23] But Byron Gassman has shown
that this concern for accuracy is not consistent, since it
creates another chronological inaccuracy.[24] In short, there
are several chronological inaccuracies throughout the
novel, and they seem to indicate a lack of concern on
Smollett's part for a detailed time scheme. My current
thinking is to reject these two changes, along with the less
important variants, as editorial or compositorial inter-
vention and follow the first edition except when it
contains an obvious error.

The procedure for editing *Travels through France and
Italy* is rather clear cut. A collation of the two London
editions of 1766 with that of 1778 reveals only compositorial variants. Luckily Smollett's copy of the first edition
with revisions, additional notes and translations of some of
the foreign quotations in his hand has survived and is now
in the British Museum — this is about as close as a Smollett
editor comes to a vision of delight. Although these
manuscript readings will be admitted into the text as
representing the author's final intentions, further emendations will have to be made, since Smollett failed to catch
a number of errors. While showing no concern whatever
for punctuation, he did make a number of minute
corrections which I would never have considered authorial
had this document not survived. Thus one will be able to
produce a highly accurate text of the *Travels*, but my joy
becomes unspeakable when I contemplate editing the texts
of *Roderick Random* and *Peregrine Pickle* with their
thousands of variants and the possibility that each variant,
no matter how minor, may have been Smollett's revision.

In most of the works just discussed, the textual editor is
dealing with only one authoritative document, and the

23. "A Consideration of the Bibliographical Problems Connected with the
First Edition of *Humphry Clinker*," *Papers of the Bibliographical Society of
America*, 44 (1950), 364-65.

24. Gassman considers the whole chronological question in his unpublished dissertation (University of Chicago, 1960), pp. 331-48. See Thomas R.
Preston's forthcoming introduction to the Iowa edition of *Humphry Clinker*.

emendation is confined to certain corrections, resolutions of ambiguities and normalization. As I have indicated earlier, the texts of *Roderick Random* and *Peregrine Pickle* present a much different problem, since both novels were revised so extensively that the textual editor is faced with choosing among thousands of substantive variants.

Since most copies of the first edition of *Roderick Random* contain two cancelled leaves correcting the text, it is likely that Smollett saw this edition through the press, and it is certainly evident that he began revising it as soon as it was printed.[25] In some copies, leaf I9 in volume one and leaf E4 in volume two are cancellans. On I9, the first page of the history of Miss Williams, Locke's name is omitted from the list of philosophers, Shaftesbury, Tindal and Hobbes, who "are remarkable for their deviation from the old way of thinking." The reason for effecting this change is not immediately apparent, but perhaps Smollett thought Locke was not radical enough, and, since he was the eighteenth century's philosophical favorite, he may have felt that the inclusion of his name would be an inconsistency jarring to the reader. The E4 cancellan is easier to explain, since it is a simple error in fact. In the original, Smollett had the Duc de Gramont killed in the Battle of Dettingen in 1743, when, in fact, he was killed at the Battle of Fontenoy, 11 May 1745. The phrase concerning the Duc de Gramont is deleted.

In spite of a heavy load of work for the booksellers, Smollett found time to make a number of imaginative changes, to polish the characterization and strengthen the style for the second edition which appeared only nine weeks after the first. Although he made fewer revisions in the second edition than he did in the third edition of 1750 and the fourth edition of 1755, the revisions of 1748 are perhaps more interesting to the student of Smollett's art, for it is clear that when he made the revisions for the third

25. See Brack and James B. Davis, "Smollett's Revisions of *Roderick Random*," *Papers of the Bibliographical Society of America*, 64 (1970), 295-311 for a more complete account.

edition he was well satisfied with the broad strokes of the novel and was concerned primarily with smoothness, clarity and grammatical fine points. It is possible that a number of the revisions for the second edition were those pointed out to him by the "best judges" whom Smollett mentions in a letter to Carlyle about December 1747 as having read the novel in manuscript.[26] In any case Smollett heightens the characterization of Tom Bowling by adding to his colorful sea dialect and increases the humor of Beau Jackson's letter from "Clayrender" by revising a number of the malapropisms. Many of the revisions, however, show the author ridding the novel of signs of haste in composition. Awkward or redundant phrases are eliminated as Smollett notes, for example, that he need not tell us that Roderick was swimming when he dragged Gawky from the water:

> plunging into a river where he was on the point of being drowned, and by the help of swimming, dragged him ashore [first edition, I, 25.24-26][27]
>
> plunging into a river where he was on the point of being drowned, dragging him ashore [second edition, I, 25.24-26]

He avoids stilted prose:

> I know not whether or not he perceived my uncle, who approached [first edition, I, 19.13-15]
>
> My uncle approached [second edition, I, 19.13-14]

and strenthens his sentences by substituting definite or concrete expressions for pronouns, abstractions, or other relatively vague constructions:

> understanding by our dialect who we were [first edition]
>
> understanding by our dialect that we were from Scotland [second edition].

Smollett often perfects satiric scenes by shifting, adding,

---

26. Knapp, p. 93.

27. Smollett returned to this passage when revising for the third edition: "plunging into a river and dragging him on shore, when he was on the point of being drowned."

or subtracting small elements; thus Strap's function as Roderick's scapegoat is far more precisely delineated by the mere addition of the contemptuous words, "with me":

> I was disgusted at this affectation, and in order to punish his hypocrisy, assured him, he might either go down to the cockpit, or stay upon the deck during the engagement [first edition, II, 321.22-23]

> I was disgusted at this affectation, and in order to punish his hypocrisy, assured him, he might take his choice either of going down to the cockpit with me, or of staying upon deck during the engagement [second edition, II, 327.22-23]

In many ways the revisions in each edition differ: many of the changes in the third edition (1750) are of a piece with those in the second (1748), as are many of those in the fourth (1755). On the whole, however, as has been mentioned above, Smollett was content in the third and fourth editions to concentrate on minor points of clarity, strength, and smoothness, and made few imaginative changes. That he does not make many important changes after the second edition seems to indicate that as an extremely rapid writer with much natural ability, he was able to express his thoughts with nearly complete success in manuscript. Some passages, however, seem to have given Smollett particular difficulty, and they reach their final state only after evolving through three or four editions:

> which deprived me of all sensation. – When I recovered [second edition, II, 7.1]

> which deprived me of all sensation. – In this deplorable situation, exposed to the rage of an incensed barbarian and the rapine of an inhuman crew, I remained for some time; and when I recovered [third edition, II, 6.13-16]

> which deprived me of all sensation. – In this deplorable situation, exposed to the rage of an incensed barbarian and the rapine of an inhuman crew, I remained for some time; and whether any disputes arose among them during the state of my annihilation, I cannot pretend to determine; but, in one particular they seemed to have been unanimous, and acted with equal dexterity and dispatch; for when I recovered [fourth edition, II, 6.13-20].

In addition to changes such as these, there are numerous minor revisions in the third and fourth editions. He winnows, for example, the frequent *whereupon*, develops a decided aversion to the word *got* ("we had got half way down" altered to "we had descended half way down"), avoids the nominative absolute ("there being only four passengers" altered to "for there were only four passengers"), and supplies missing pronoun references ("this" "this expedient"; "which having done" altered to "which operation I having performed").

The full extent of Smollett's care in revising *Roderick Random* will not be known until the publication of this volume, but a rough numerical estimate indicates that, in the second edition, in volume one, substantive changes average one in every two pages; in volume two, more than one in every three pages. In the other two revised editions there is an average of about one substantive change per page, with slightly more substantive changes in the fourth edition. All the revisions show a stylistic meticulousness not generally associated with Smollett this early in his career.[28]

It has long been known that *Peregrine Pickle* was revised extensively for the second edition of 1758. Though Smollett scholars are given an adequate representation of the kinds of revisions made for the second edition in Buck's *Study in Smollett*, they are not given, as I mentioned earlier, proper indication of the extent of the

28. There are several studies of Smollett's earlier prose style, Albrecht B. Strauss, "On Smollett's Language: A Paragraph in *Ferdinand Count Fathom*," *English Institute Essays, 1958* (New York, 1959), pp. 25-54; Philip Stevick, "Stylistic Energy in the Early Smollett," *Studies in Philology*, 64 (1967), 712-19; and Stuart Miller, *The Picaresque Novel* (Cleveland, 1967), esp. pp. 122-27, but none of them takes into account any of the author's revisions. Smollett's later prose style has been discussed in some detail. Buck in *A Study in Smollett*, pp. 11-19, discusses his revisions for the second edition of *Peregrine Pickle* (1758), although some of his conclusions must be modified by the evidence presented below. Louis L. Martz in *The Later Career of Tobias Smollett* (New Haven, 1942) analyzes the development of his prose style after 1753 and deals with the earlier style only by implication. See also Paul-Gabriel Boucé, *Les Romans de Smollett* (Paris, 1971), pp. 392-431.

revisions. Buck caught almost all of the major deletions, failing to note only that of the episode in Chapter XVIII in which Perry plays a joke on Jolter by having Pipes impersonate the maid whom the tutor had hoped to bed. But apart from these major revisions, Buck's collation is extremely poor. He failed to realize that his copy of volume three of the first edition had leaf L12 in the cancelled state, and so missed a rather extended revision which was made, presumably, during the printing of the first edition. Of the numerous and detailed substantive variants such as those just discussed in *Roderick Random*, Buck recorded fewer than half. In his collation of volume two, for example, he lists a variant on 252.7-8; the next variant recorded is on 266.15. In fact, there are at least ten substantive variants on the intervening pages. A typical instance can be seen on page 170 of volume two. Buck has noted that at 170.1 (160.23, second edition) Smollett has broken a long sentence into two shorter ones, and at 170.36 (161.22, second edition) "This benefaction" has become "The benefaction," but he has not noted that at 170.22-23 (161.8-9, second edition) "walking round the ramparts, with a view of enjoying some private conversation" becomes "walking round the ramparts. He hoped to enjoy some private conversation" and at 170.31-32 (161.17-19, second edition) "that ecclesiastick, which he was obliged to purchase with another purse, that he offered" becomes "that ecclesiastick. This he was obliged to purchase with another purse, which he offered. . . ." Buck, on the basis of his collation, believes the revisions of the novel to be "essentially one of those factory products."

> Allowing for Smollett's greater personal interest in his own work, and better opinion of it, his method of revising *Peregrine* was probably fairly characteristic of his regular hack methods.
> In hack-work expediency is the watch word. In the revision of *Peregrine*, nine parts are expedience and one part literary art. The former was done in deference to other people's opinion; the latter must have been done to please

himself. . . .[29]

Most critics would agree that Smollett's greatest weakness as a novelist was a deficient sense of form, particularly in this novel, with its insertion of the "Memoirs of a Lady of Quality" and the extensive excision of passages, such as the bitter personal attacks on Garrick and Fielding, which Smollett must have found embarrassing by 1757. Whatever his failures in structure, they do not make him a less conscious literary artist. I think that when the full extent of the revisions is made known, it will be difficult to dismiss them as a product of Smollett's "factory." Although it is true that many alterations here, as well as those in *Roderick Random*, do show some signs of haste and carelessness, their comprehensiveness and attention to detail reveal the author as an artist very much concerned with the particulars of his art.

Since critics have concerned themselves so long with Smollett's various kinds of "offensiveness" or "tastelessness," it will be worth while to examine briefly some of the changes made in *Roderick Random* and *Peregrine Pickle* in this light. There were no passages suppressed in *Roderick Random*, of course, and the revisions are confined to changing a few words of questionable taste, and these words were not changed consistently. It is easy to see that Smollett would want Miss Jenny to say "louse" instead of "f--t" and Beau Jackson to say, more appropriately, "agad" for "by G-d," but it is more difficult to understand why he would soften the language of such characters as Mr. Crab, Rifle and Weazel. Smollett also seems to have developed an aversion to swearing *by* God though he is not bothered by *oons* and *ods* and various other blasphemous forms. Why Smollett changed some words and left others is far from clear.

29. Pp. 18-19. Buck does not make clear what he means by "regular hack methods." Whatever they might be, they probably do not include revising works for which one receives no money, since the time could be better spent producing a new work. Buck was unaware of Smollett's numerous revisions for *Roderick Random*.

Moreover, even though he went to some trouble to make changes in *Roderick Random*, he certainly did not bother to avoid coarse language when he composed *Peregrine Pickle*. Little of the language was softened and, while a number of passages of doubtful taste are removed and others revised, many passages remain. Smollett's statement in the Advertisement to the second edition of *Peregrine Pickle* (1758) that "he flattered himself, that he has expunged every adventure, phrase, and insinuation that could be construed by the most delicate reader into a trespass upon the rules of decorum" has been taken much too seriously by critics who have tested this statement against their own standards of nineteenth- or twentieth-century taste and have found it wanting. It seems much better to take Smollett's statement in good faith and consider the apparent discrepancy between the statement and the revisions as a difference in taste rather than as a failure of imagination on Smollett's part.

In *Roderick Random* the textual editor is dealing with four different forms of the text. The first edition will be used as copy-text, its accidentals will be retained, and the revised readings from the second, third and fourth editions will be admitted into the text once their authority has been determined. This procedure is straightforward enough and is complicated only by the enormous number of substantive variants and the usual large gray area of indifferent readings, the kind that Smollett could have made deliberately but that compositors frequently make through carelessness, as when "paper, pen and ink" in one edition become "pen, ink, and paper" in another.

The problem facing the editor in choosing an editorial procedure for *Peregrine Pickle* is much different. The normal editorial procedure would be to choose the first edition as copy to emend, retain its accidentals, and admit authoritative revisions from the second edition. The major difficulty in following this procedure is that the approximately 80 pages of material that Smollett deleted for the second edition could not be admitted into the text and would have to remain in the table of rejected readings. The question is this: Is it better to retain the 80 pages of deleted material and reject the numerous stylistic revisions made for the second edition, many of which, no doubt, improve the text, or is it better to retain the stylistic revisions and relegate the deleted episodes to an appendix? To retain the rejected episodes of the first edition while admitting the stylistic revisions made for the second edition would set editorial theory back to the nineteenth century and the "best reading" theory of emendation so eloquently dismissed by A. E. Housman[30] and numerous other editorial practitioners since. While the theoretical grounds are interesting and received a great deal of thought, the very practical consideration that the audience for which this edition is intended would prefer to have Smollett's text in its most important form with all of the deletions in the text determined my method. This text, now being edited by D. H. Stefanson, will contain all of the stylistic revisions made for the second edition with the deleted passages also included and duly marked by some method, to be worked out in conjunction with the designer of the volume, so that the reader will immediately know that this was one of the passages deleted in the second edition without having to go to the back of the volume to consult the textual tables. This compromise will solve several problems: it will make the volume easier to read, it will reduce greatly the size of the textual apparatus, and it will allow the volume editor to annotate the passage if necessary.

Here are a few reasons why our edition has taken longer than planned, and there are many more that could be discussed — if *time* permitted. There is always the question of the exact audience for the edition and how this will affect not only the handling of the text but the introductions and explanatory notes as well. The answer is

30. "Preface to *Manilius I* (1903)," *Selected Prose*, ed. John Carter (Cambridge, 1961), pp. 35-39. See also Brack, Introduction to Brack and Barnes, pp. 3-6, 14-16.

simple in theory but difficult in practice, and an almost incalcuable amount of time is spent trying to determine what is to be annotated and how; the volume editor, the general editor and the editorial board rarely agree on these matters.[31] It is complicated somewhat in this edition by the variety of the works: novels, plays, poems, travels and a political satire. Then there is the loss of key personnel; in this case the death of my friend, Curt Zimansky, who voluntarily assumed the duties of secretary of the editorial board and gave unselfishly of his time and energies and without whose wisdom and good humor we would have all given up in despair years ago. In short, the possibilities for confusion and delay are endless: notes can be stolen from trunks of automobiles, and it is possible to knock off six weeks to write a paper for an editorial conference explaining why your edition has been delayed. Johnson has summed up the problem best: "A large work is difficult because it is large"

> and every work is lengthened by a thousand causes that can, and ten thousand that cannot, be recounted. Perhaps no extensive and multifarious performance was ever effected within the term originally fixed in the undertaker's mind. He that runs against Time, has an antagonist not subject to casualties.

But the Preacher hath the final words of wisdom: "Better *is* the end of a thing than the beginning thereof."

---

31. "Grant I have mastered learning's crabbed text,/ Still there's the comment."

# Members of the Conference

Marcia Allentuck, *City University of New York*
John Baird, *Victoria College, University of Toronto*
Warner Barnes, *University of Texas at Austin*
Martin Battistin, *University of Virginia*
Elizabeth B. Bentley, *Toronto*
G. E. Bentley, Jr., *University College, University of Toronto*
David Blewett, *McMaster University*
O M Brack, Jr., *Arizona State University*
William J. Cameron, *University of Western Ontario*
John Carroll, *University College, University of Toronto*
Mrs. John Carroll, *Toronto*
Brian Corman, *Erindale College, University of Toronto*
Richard A. Davies, *Acadia University*
Eric W. Domville, *New College, University of Toronto*
James Downey, *Carleton University*
Donald D. Eddy, *Cornell University*
David G. Esplin, *University of Toronto Library*
Byron Gassman, *Brigham Young University*
J. C. Goslin, *Mt. Clemens, Michigan*
Ronald Hafter, *Dalhousie University*

Francess G. Halpenny, *University of Toronto*
Sandra E. Harris, *Mills Memorial Library, McMaster University*
Claudia C. Haug, *Ann Arbor, Michigan*
Thomas H. Haug, *Ann Arbor, Michigan*
Patricia Hernlund, *Wayne State University*
J. Howard, *Scarborough College, University of Toronto*
Roderick Huang, *University of Windsor*
Arlene Jackson, *St. Joseph's College, Philadelphia*
Heather Jackson, *Scarborough College, University of Toronto*
Eugene Joliat, *University College, University of Toronto*
Ellen Keller, *Case Western Reserve University*
William Kinsley, *Université de Montréal*
Anne Lancashire, *University College, University of Toronto*
Richard Landon, *University of Toronto Library*
Roger Laufer, *Université de Paris*
Richard Loney, *Toronto*
Richard N. Lutes, *Detroit*
Robert S. Matteson, *St. Lawrence University*
T. Maynard, *Simon Fraser University*
John McClelland, *Victoria College, University of Toronto*
George F. McFarland, *St. Lawrence University*
Michael H. Millgate, *University College, University of Toronto*
J. P. Moore CSB, *Pontifical Institute of Mediaeval Studies*
Charles C. Murrah, *University of Windsor*
Melvyn New, *University of Flordia*
Richard Proudfoot, *University of Virginia*
A. R. Pugh, *University of New Brunswick*
Derek V. Robertson, *Mills Memorial Library, McMaster University*
Carole Royer, *Wayne State University*
D. W. Smith, *Victoria College, University of Toronto*
John Stedmond, *Queen's University*
Clarence Tracy, *University College, University of Toronto*
Prudence Tracy, *University of Toronto Press*

Edward Watson, *University of Windsor*
R. M. Wiles, *McMaster Universtiy*
Jean L. Wilson, *University of Toronto Press*
James Woodruff, *University of Western Ontario*
Ruth A. Zaleski, *Wayne State University*

# Index